E-Z Play TODAY chord notation is designed for playing **standard chord positions** or **single key chords** on all **major brand organs** and **electronic keyboards.**

This publication is not for sale in
the EC and/or Australia
or New Zealand.

7777 W. BLUEMOUND RD. P.O. BOX 13819 MILWAUKEE, WI 53213

# Contents

# The Fifties

## by Stanley Green

*President Dwight D. Eisenhower*

*Gen. Douglas MacArthur*

Bracketed by the Korean War at the beginning of the decade and the increasing American involvement in the Vietnam War at the end, the Fifties are recalled largely as a period of relative tranquility. With the country presided over by the avuncular presence of Dwight D. Eisenhower for eight of the decade's years, it was a time in which people believed in the Power of Positive Thinking, were shocked at the goings on in Peyton Place, and adopted as a symbol of the age the status-seeking, buttoned-down Man in the Grey Flannel Suit. There was also a feeling, reflecting both confidence and relief, that the United States was somehow able to get through crisis after crisis without the cold war turning into a global carnage.

Of course, there were serious conflicts and confrontations. The Korean War, which lasted from the summer of 1950 to the summer of 1953 almost involved the country in a full-scale war after Chinese Communist forces had overrun the 38th parallel in an effort to aid the North Koreans. This action resulted in General Douglas MacArthur's threat of massive retaliation which, in turn, resulted in the General's removal by President Harry S. Truman. The Kefauver Senate Committee investigated the farflung activities of organized crime in the full glare of television cameras. NATO — the North Atlantic Treaty Organization — approved a European army to defend the continent against the possibility of a Soviet attack. Senator Joe McCarthy conducted his witch hunt against subversives in government (for which he was later censured by the Senate), thereby introducing the term McCarthyism into the language. Juvenile delinquency — known as "JD" — was on the rise. The Soviet Union sent its tanks into Hungary to quell a rebellion against Communist rule which cost the lives of 32,000 freedom fighters. Racial unrest in the South was accellerated by the Supreme Court's decision that segregated schools were unconstitutional, and federal troops had to be dispatched to Little Rock and other cities.

*Frank Sinatra*

The decade, however, could be proud of many notable achievements in a variety of fields. Television, which had become the major source of home entertainment in the late Forties, was now available in color and could be transmitted coast to coast. Sir Edmund Hillary and his guide, Tenzing Norkay, were the first to reach the top of Mt. Everest. The Nautilus became the first atom-powered submarine. Dr. Jonas Salk perfected the vaccine against polio. Martin Luther King Jr. led the successful boycott of Montgomery, Alabama. Van Cliburn, of Kilgore, Texas, became the first American to win the Tschaikowsky Prize in the Soviet Union's international piano competition. And the United States launched its first man-made satellite into orbit.

Assorted diversions, fads, scandals, and other pleasures also preoccupied our time. The mambo and the cha-cha brought the Latin beat to the nation's dance halls. Quiz shows abounded on television, and Davy Crockett hats became the rage among youngsters throughout the country. Though the marriage of Grace Kelly of Philadelphia and Prince Rainier of Monaco was unquestionably the wedding of the decade, the period also saw the celebrated knot-tying — and eventual untying — of Frank Sinatra and Ava Gardner, Marilyn Monroe and both Joe DiMaggio and Arthur Miller, Debbie Reynolds and Eddie Fisher, and Elizabeth Taylor and Eddie Fisher.

*A*s befitting the general mood, the music scene found romantic expressions dominant in the Fifties, whether played by orchestras or sung by balladeers. Most of the instrumental hits, in fact, even featured lush, quasi-symphonic arrangements to decorate such pieces as Leroy Anderson's "Blue Tango," Victor Young's "Around the World" (the composer's theme from the film of the same name), and Hugo Winterhalter's "Canadian Sunset." And then there was the phenomenon known as "mood music."

*B*ut primarily the decade offered a varied collection of soloists singing their hearts out about the joys and pains of requited and unrequited love. Each, of course, had his or her special sound. There was the kittenish purr of Eartha Kitt ("C'est Si Bon"), the roughedged sincerity of Tony Bennett ("Blue Velvet"), the leathery

powerhouse of Frankie Laine ("I Believe"), the open-throttled range of Kay Starr ("Wheel of Fortune"), the All-American boyishness of Eddie Fisher ("Oh! My Pa-pa"), the effortless warmth of singing rage Patti Page ("Old Cape Cod"), the high-pitched intensity of Johnny Mathis ("Misty," "Wonderful! Wonderful!"), and the creamy intimacy of Nat "King" Cole ("Unforgettable," "That's All," "When I Fall in Love"). From the movies came two of the nation's favorite girls next door, Doris Day with "Que Sera Sera" (featured in *The Man Who Knew Too Much*) and Debbie Reynolds with "Tammy" (featured in *Tammy and the Bachelor*). And veterans Bing Crosby and Frank Sinatra continued to be in the forefront of our master song stylists. Crosby had a winner in Cole Porter's "True Love" (which he sang in the film *High Society*), and Sinatra had winners in "Three Coins in the Fountain" (which he sang on the film's soundtrack) and "Young at Heart." It should also be noted that the Fifties were awash with lachrymal expressions, notably "Cry" (a Johnnie Ray trademark), "Cry Me a River" (Julie London's first hit), and "Crying in the Chapel."

The earliest indication that changes were about to become evident in the musical taste of the country was the mid-Fifties success of two rock-and-roll items, "Rock Around the Clock" and "Shake, Rattle and Roll," both introduced and popularized by Bill Haley and the Comets. But the singer who most influenced the shape and direction of American pop music was the swivel-hipped, flamboyant Elvis Presley, who won over a new generation to the rockabilly sound of "Blue Suede Shoes," "Don't Be Cruel," "Heartbreak Hotel," and "All Shook Up."

During this period there were also a number of songs — or at least their melodies — that were exhumed from the past. Perhaps the one that went back the farthest was the sentimental ballad "Love Me Tender," another Presley hit, which was known as "Aura Lee" when it was first published in 1861, and later as "Army Blue" when it became a favorite of West Point cadets. "Tom Dooley," the Kingston Trio's chart buster which started a brief vogue for folkish numbers, began life in a North Carolina prison in 1868. There a murderer named Thomas C. Dula penned the threnody about his foul deed, though his name became somewhat altered through the years. "The Glow Worm" dates back to 1902 when, as *"Glühwürmchen,"* it was sung in a German operetta. Its catchy staccato tune made it a perennial barbershop favorite, but it was not until 1952, when aided by a new lyric by Johnny Mercer, that it became one of the Mills Brothers' most requested selections.

*Elvis Presley*

and "They Call the Wind Maria" (pronounced "ma-rī-a"). Then they went on to electrify Broadway with *My Fair Lady,* their acclaimed adaptation of Shaw's *Pygmalion,* whence came the ardent ballad "On the Street Where You Live." Cole Porter was back with *Can-Can,* his next to last big hit, which featured the hymn to the city of lights called "I Love Paris." Prolific composer Jule Styne had two long-run shows in the Fifties. With co-lyricists Betty Comden and Adolph Green he penned *Bells Are Ringing* as a showcase for Judy Holliday to sing, among others, the rueful piece "The Party's Over," and with lyricist Stephen Sondheim he created the songs for the show-business saga *Gypsy,* with Ethel Merman scoring with the pulse-pounding "Everything's Coming Up Roses."

When "It's All in the Game" was enjoying popularity in the early Fifties, few realized that it had been written in 1912 as an instrumental violin piece called "Melody." Even fewer realized that its composer was Charles G. Dawes, a banker and diplomat, who served as Vice President of the United States under Calvin Coolidge. Charles Chaplin's "Smile," which he composed as the theme for his 1936 silent film *Modern Times,* was another melody that was outfitted with new lyrics in the Fifties and turned into a song hit. It was also in 1936 that the legendary Leadbelly (né Hudder Ledbetter) recorded his "Goodnight, Irene" for the Library of Congress while serving time in the Louisiana State Prison; fourteen years later the Weavers, with Gordon Jenkins' orchestra, made a recording that finally helped it win popular favor. Merle Travis wrote and recorded his cynical protest song "Sixteen Tons" in 1947, then had to wait eight years for Tennessee Ernie Ford to reintroduce it on radio and send it spinning high on the charts.

*Ethel Merman in "Gypsy"*

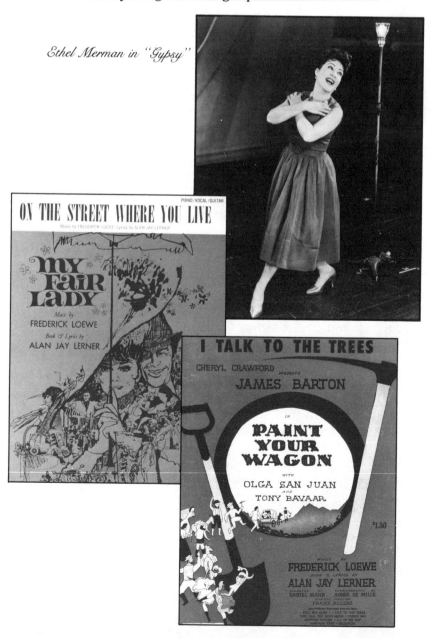

Songs from Broadway during the Fifties continued to provide the pop music market with some of its most durable standards. The relatively new team of lyricist Alan Jay Lerner and composer Frederick Loewe had their second stage success with *Paint Your Wagon,* a tale of the California gold rush, whose score included "I Talk to the Trees"

And the old masters Rodgers and Hammerstein capped their partnership with *The Sound of Music,* written for Mary Martin. "Climb Ev'ry Mountain" was their inspirational piece that gave courage to the members of the Trapp family as they set out over the Alps to escape the pursuing Nazis.

The serenity of the Fifties, however, was not to last. As the decade came to a close, Americans still seemed optimistic and self-satisfied. But still there was an ongoing problem about what to do about stemming Communist expansion in a tiny country in Southeast Asia. And it showed no signs of being solved...

*Rodgers & Hammerstein*

*Mary Martin in*
*"The Sound Of Music"*

# All I Have To Do Is Dream

Registration 2
Rhythm: Slow Rock or Fox Trot

By Boudleaux Bryant

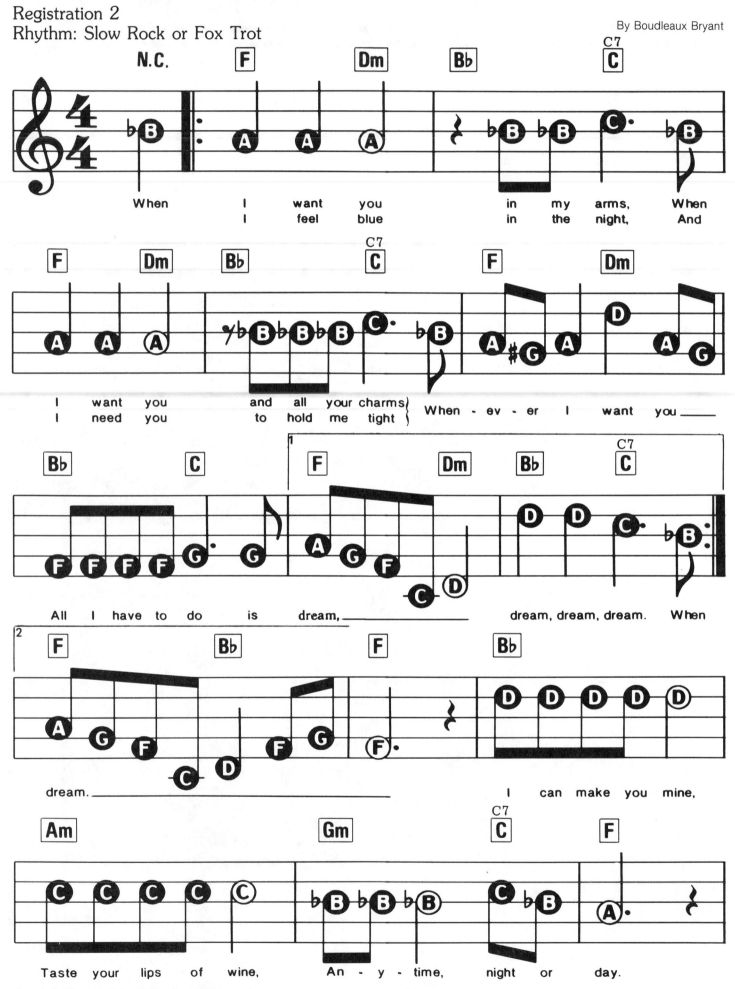

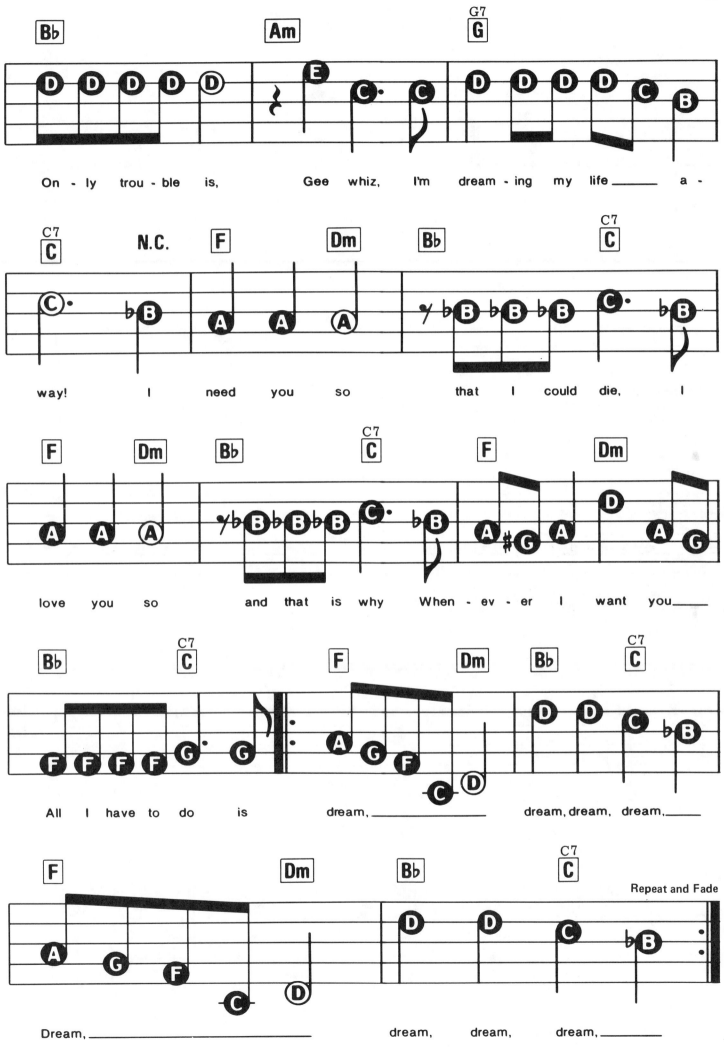

# All Shook Up

Registration 5
Rhythm: Rock

Words and Music by
Otis Blackwell and Elvis Presley

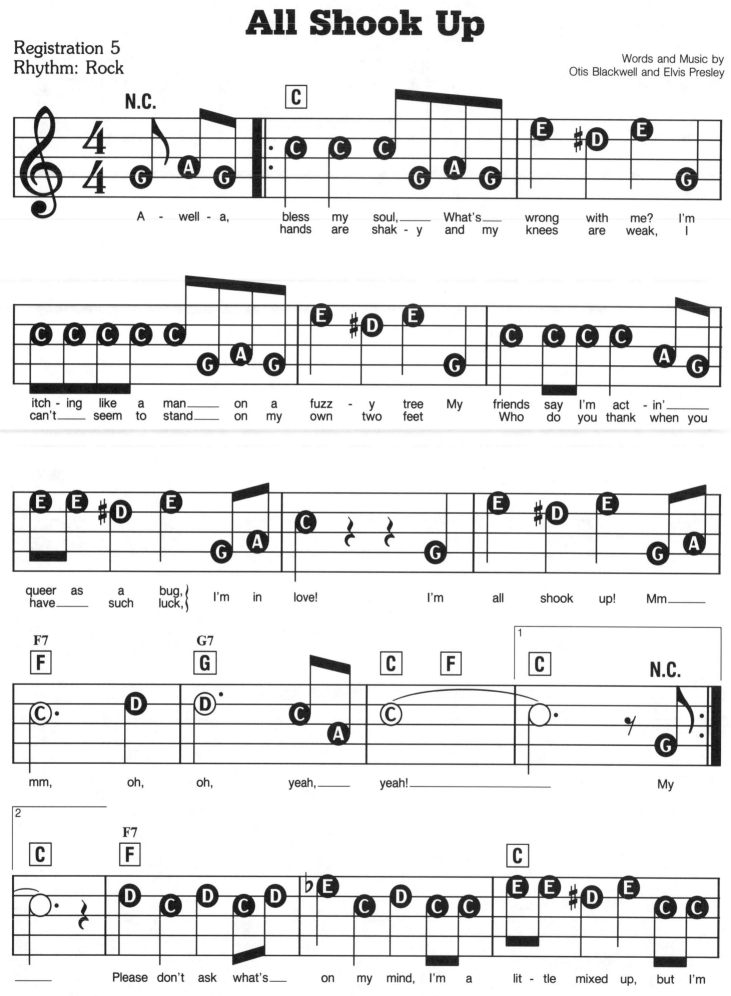

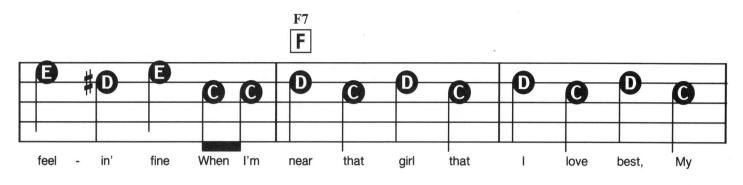

feel - in' fine When I'm near that girl that I love best, My

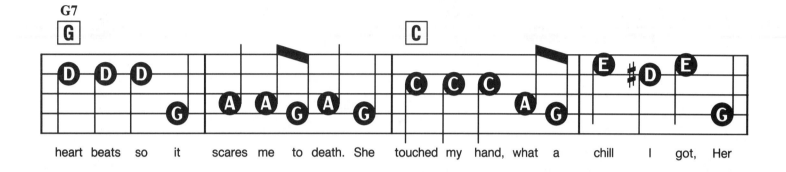

heart beats so it scares me to death. She touched my hand, what a chill I got, Her

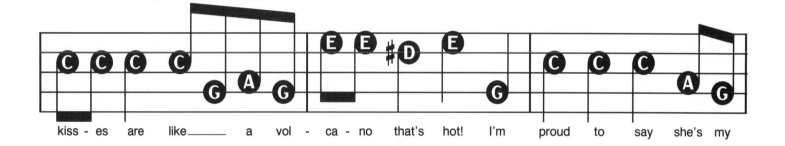

kiss - es are like_____ a vol - ca - no that's hot! I'm proud to say she's my

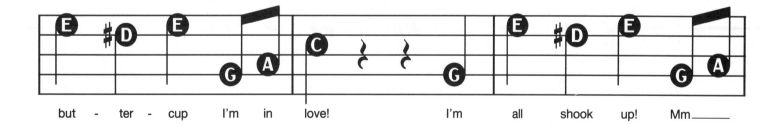

but - ter - cup I'm in love! I'm all shook up! Mm_____

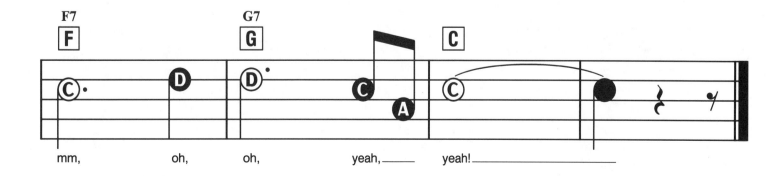

mm, oh, oh, yeah,_____ yeah!_____

# Around The World

Registration 5
Rhythm: Waltz

Words and Music by Victor Young
and Harold Adamson

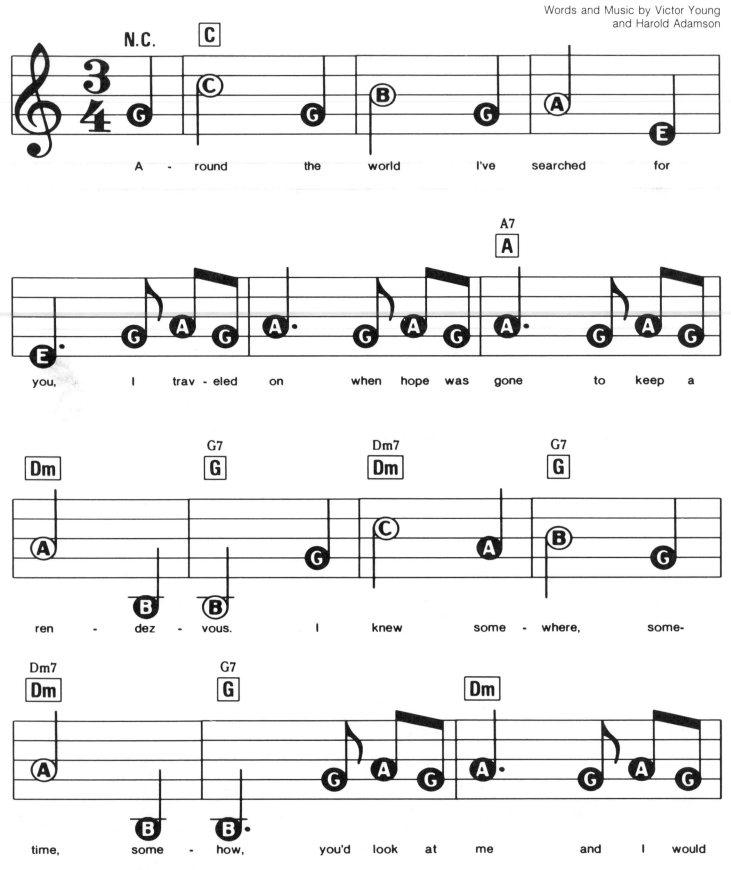

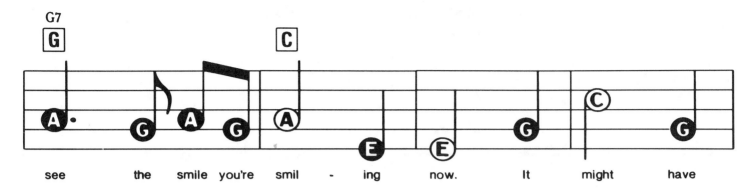

see the smile you're smil - ing now. It might have

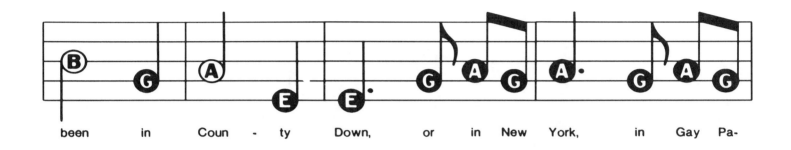

been in Coun - ty Down, or in New York, in Gay Pa-

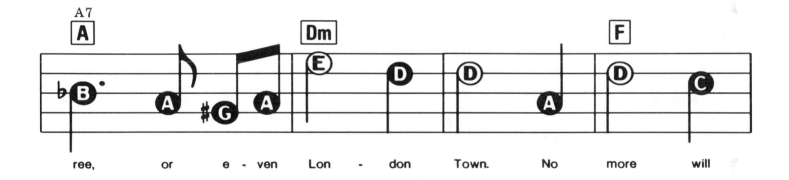

ree, or e - ven Lon - don Town. No more will

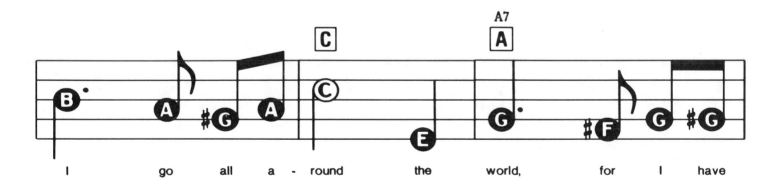

I go all a - round the world, for I have

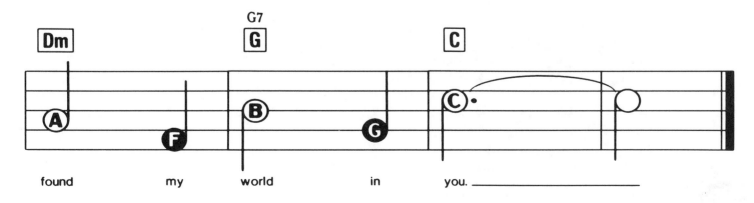

found my world in you. _____

# Arrivederci Roma
## (From the Motion Picture "SEVEN HILLS OF ROME")

Registration 3
Rhythm: Latin

Words by Carl Sigman
Music by R. Rascel

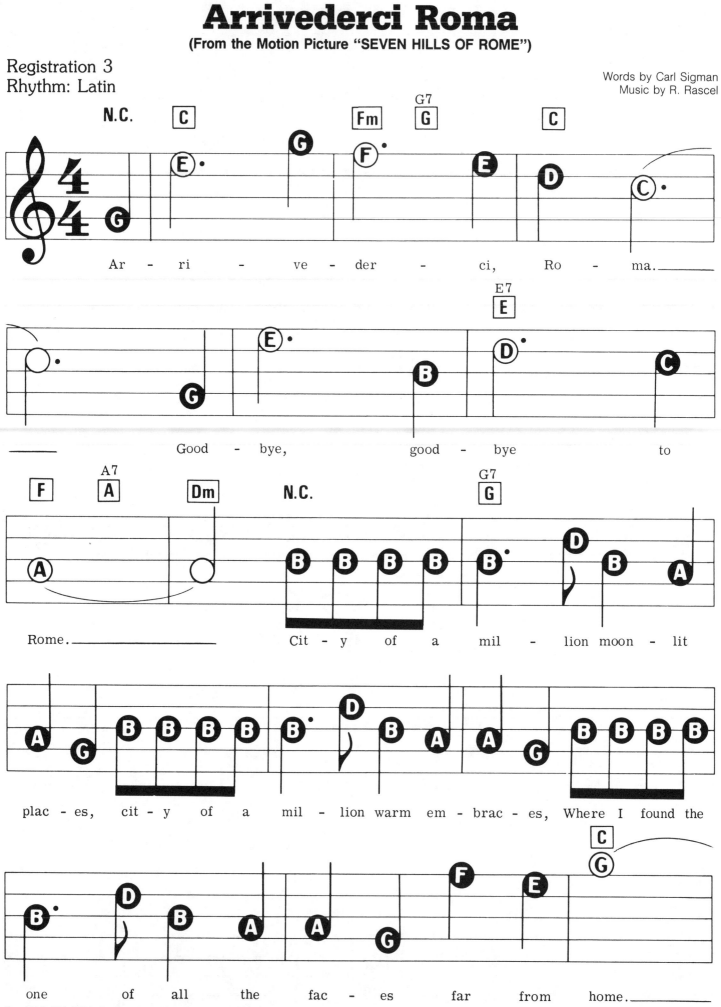

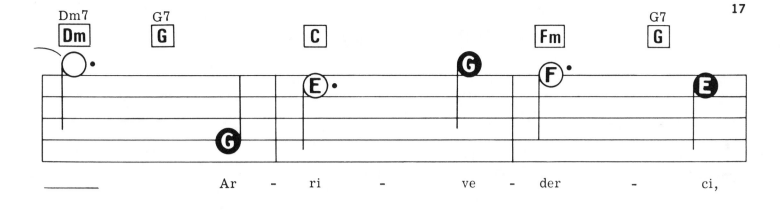

_____ Ar - ri - ve - der - ci,

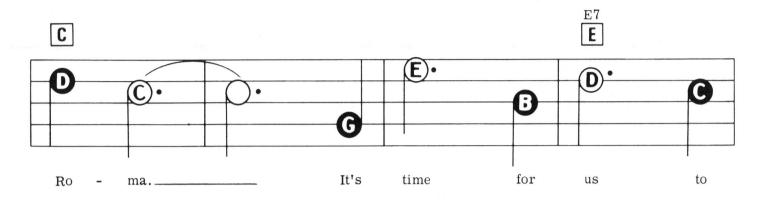

Ro - ma._____ It's time for us to

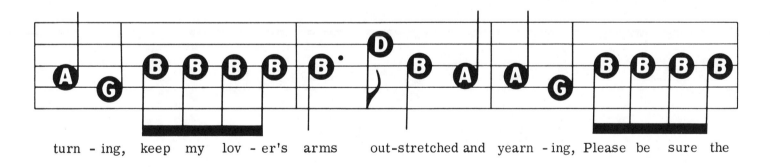

part._____ Save the wed - ding bells for my re -

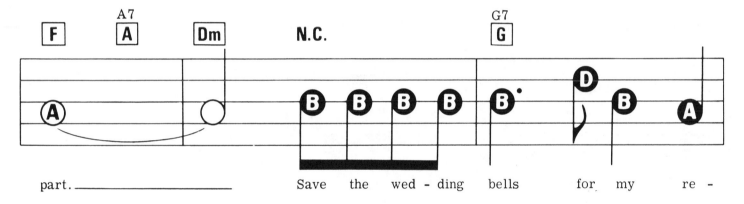

turn - ing, keep my lov - er's arms out-stretched and yearn - ing, Please be sure the

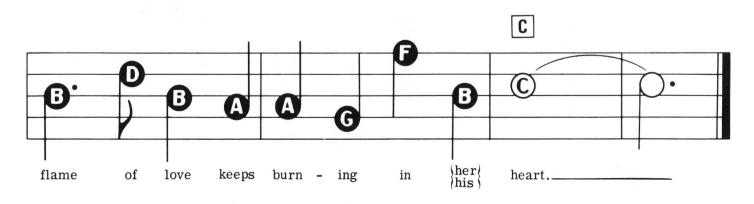

flame of love keeps burn - ing in {her/his} heart._____

# At The Hop

Registration 5
Rhythm: Rock

Words and Music by Arthur Singer,
John Medora and David White

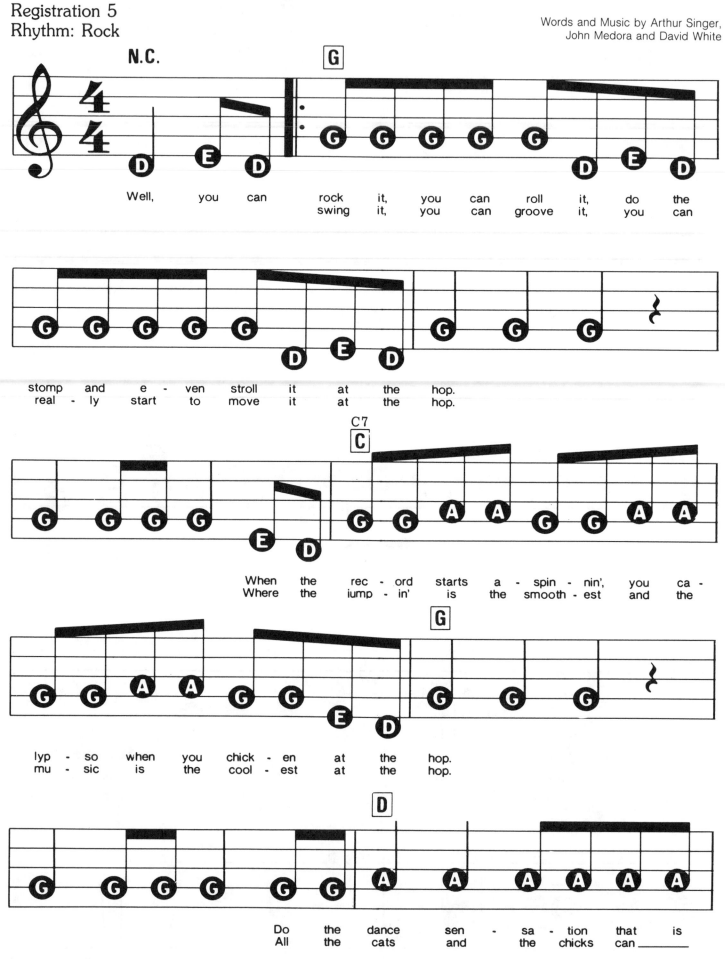

Well, you can rock it, you can roll it, do the
swing it, you can can groove it, do you can

stomp and e-ven stroll it at the hop.
real-ly start to move it at the hop.

When the rec-ord starts a-spin-nin', you ca-
Where the jump-in' is the smooth-est and the

lyp-so when you chick-en at the hop.
mu-sic is the cool-est at the hop.

Do the dance sen-sa-tion that is
All the cats and the chicks can _____

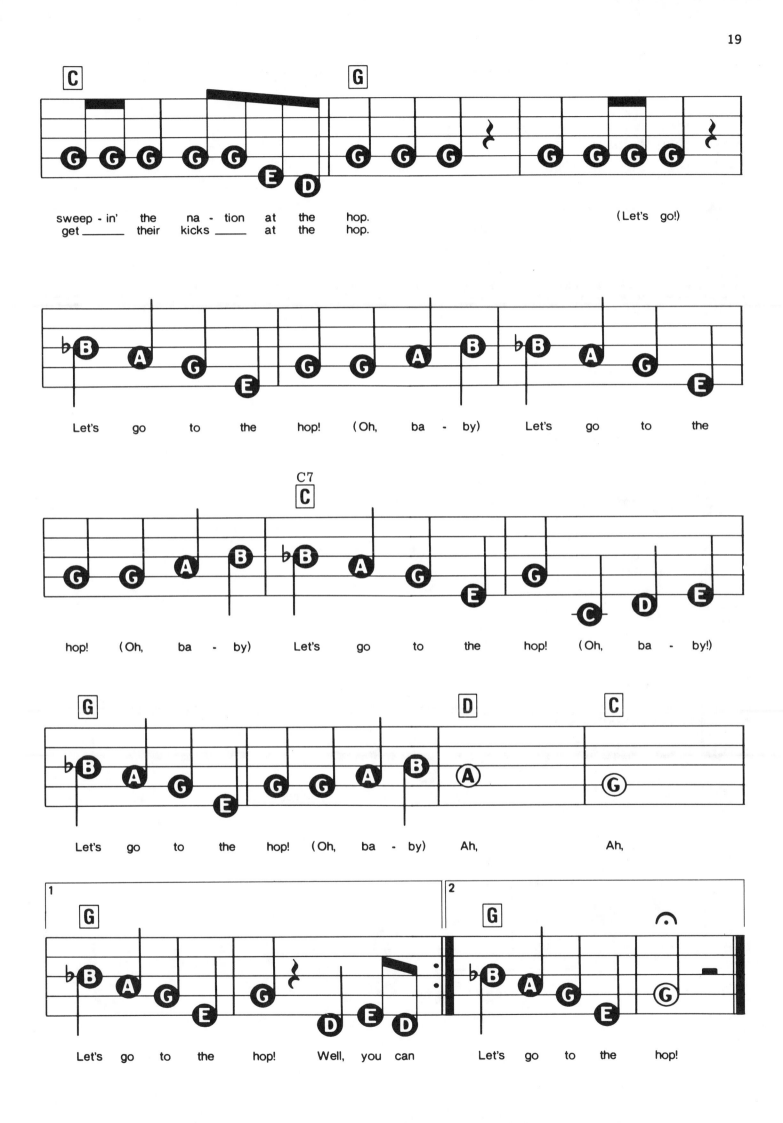

# The Ballad Of Davy Crockett

Registration 2
Rhythm: Fox Trot or Swing

Words by Tom Blackburn
Music by George Bruns

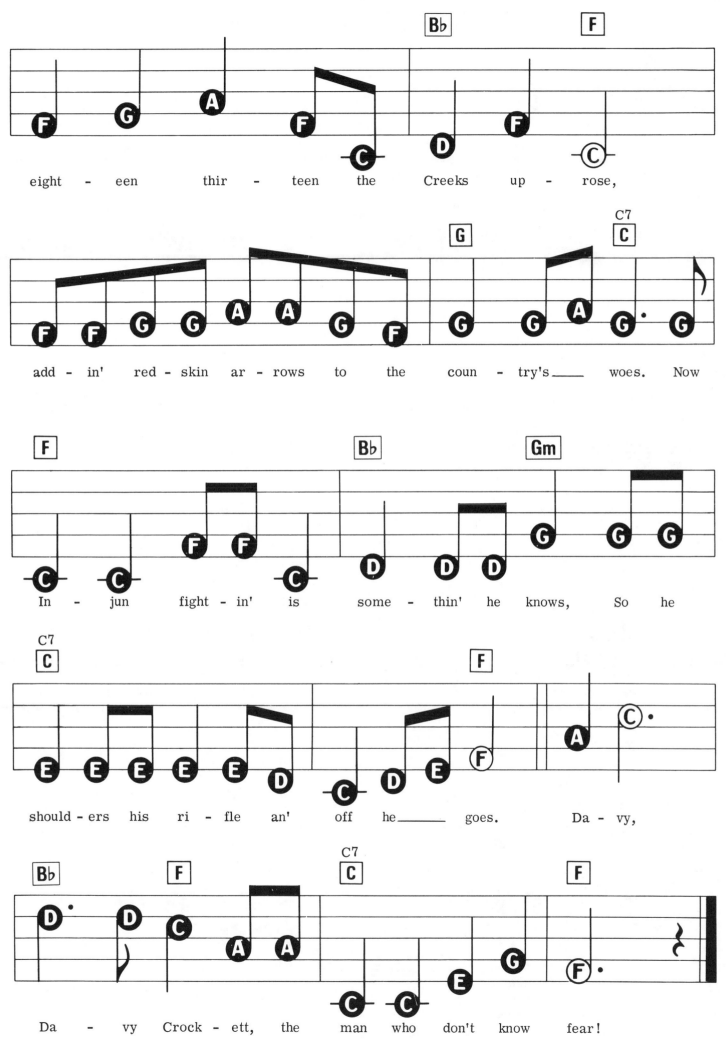

21

# Blue Suede Shoes

Registration 5
Rhythm: Rock

Words and Music by
Carl Lee Perkins

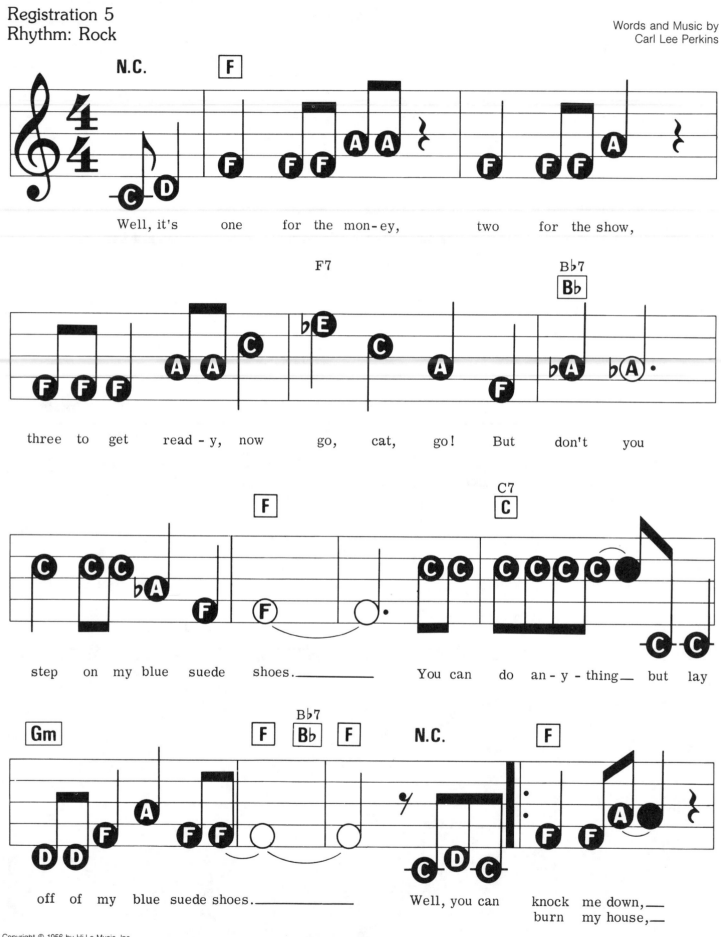

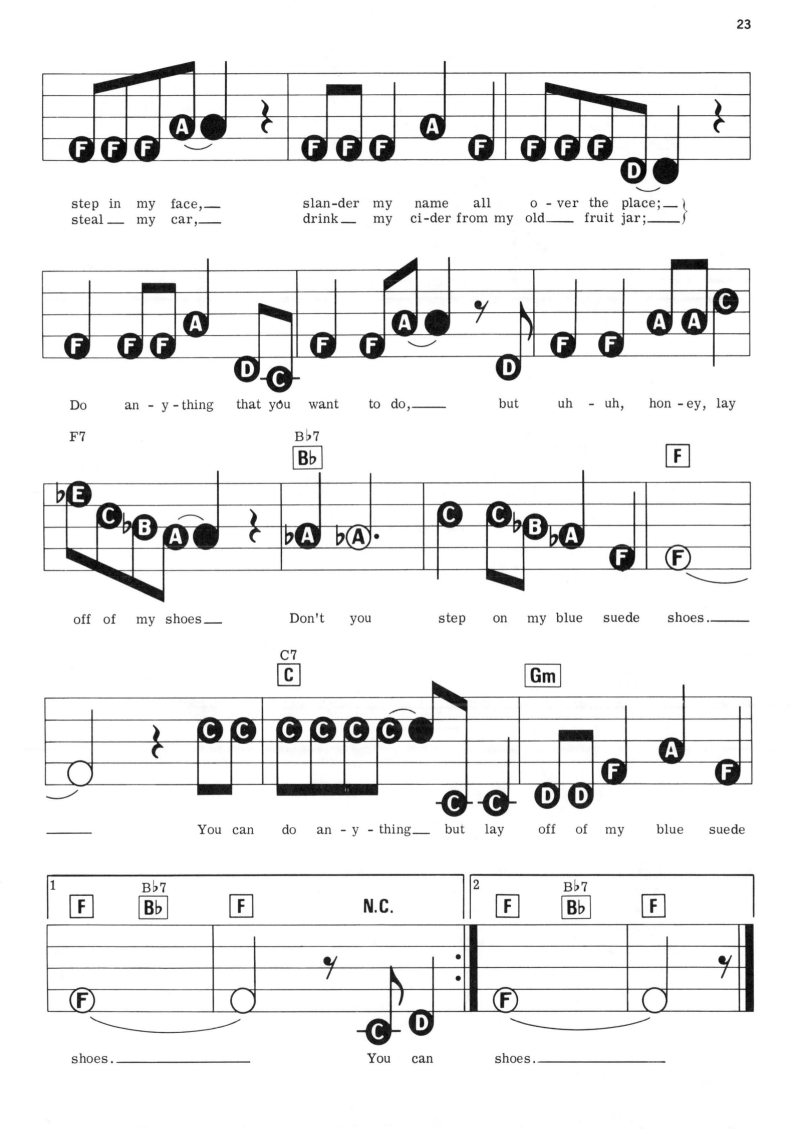

# Blue Velvet

Registration 1
Rhythm: Fox Trot or Swing

Words and Music by
Bernie Wayne and Lee Morris

# Blue Velvet

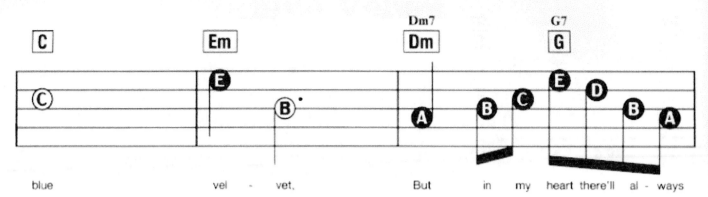

blue         vel - vet,      But   in  my  heart there'll al - ways

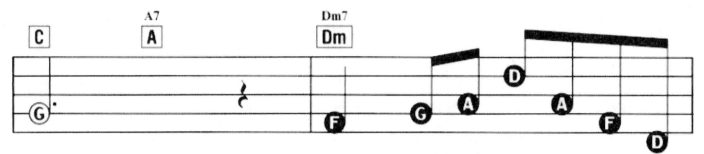

be,        Pre - cious  and  warm  a  mem - o -

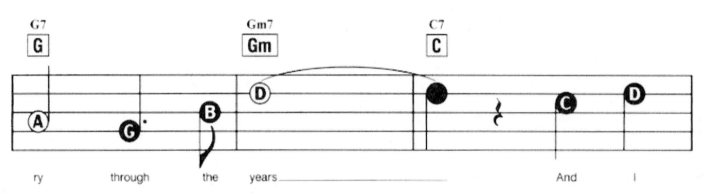

ry     through    the    years         And    I

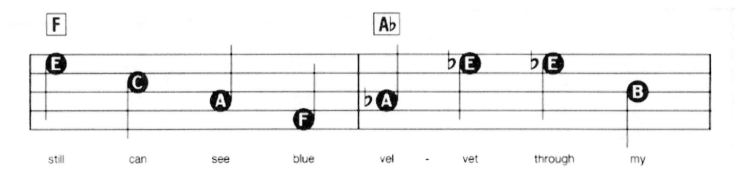

still     can     see     blue    vel - vet   through    my

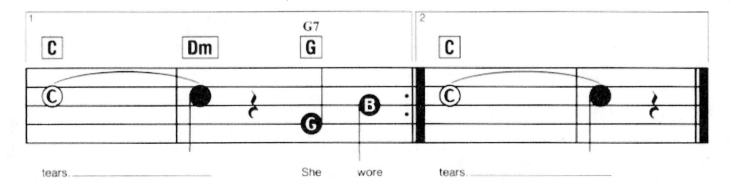

tears.            She  wore   tears.

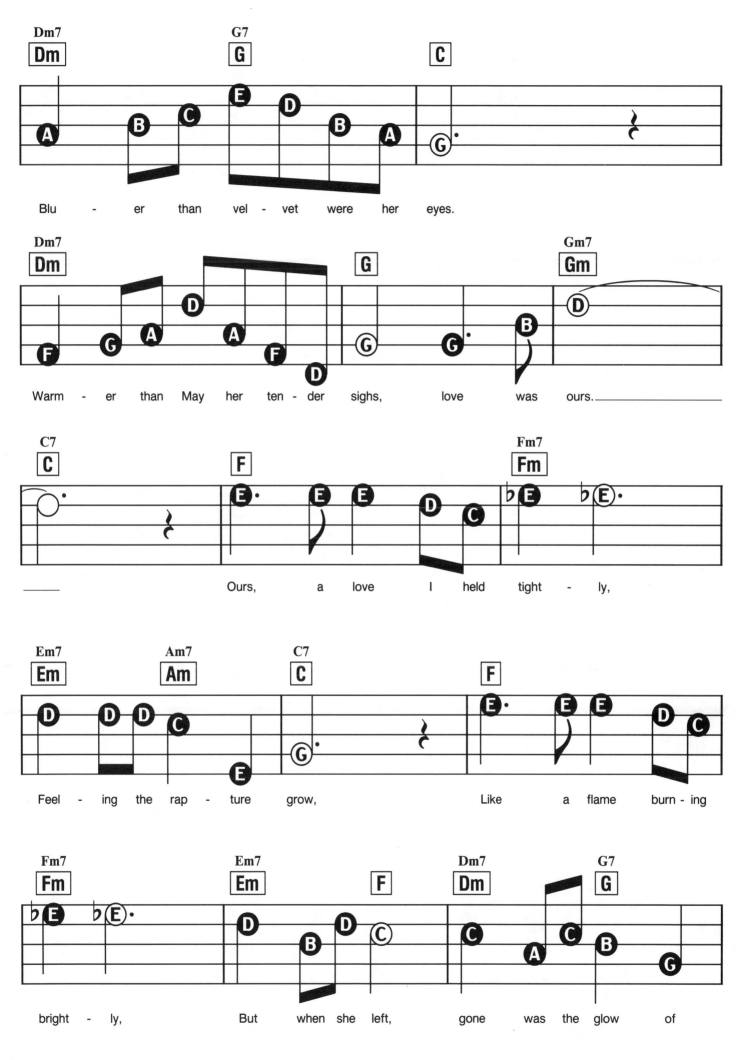

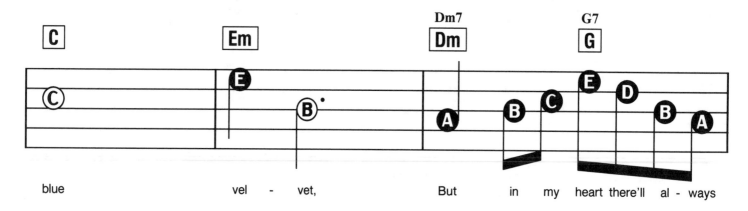

blue                    vel - vet,        But      in    my   heart there'll  al - ways

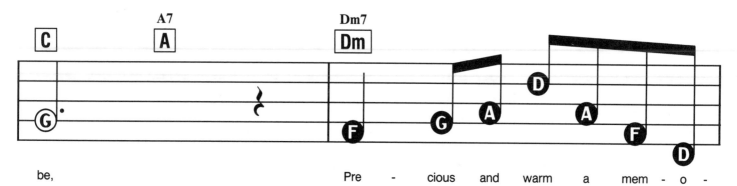

be,                          Pre  -  cious   and   warm   a   mem - o -

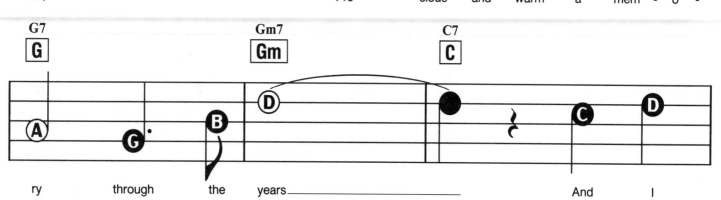

ry        through      the    years_____        And        I

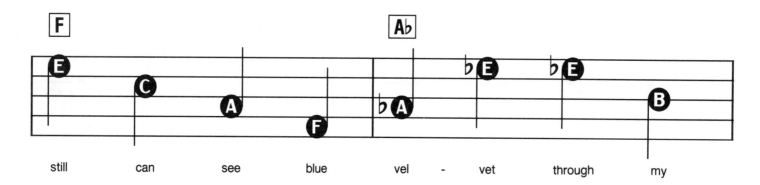

still       can        see       blue      vel  -  vet    through     my

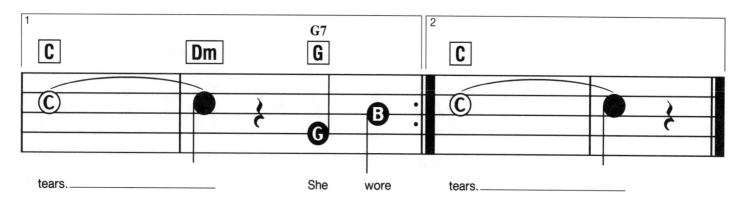

tears._____          She   wore    tears._____

# The Glow Worm

Modern Version by Johnny Mercer
Original Lyric by Lilla Cayley Robinson
Music by Paul Lincke

Registration 4
Rhythm: Fox Trot or Cha-Cha

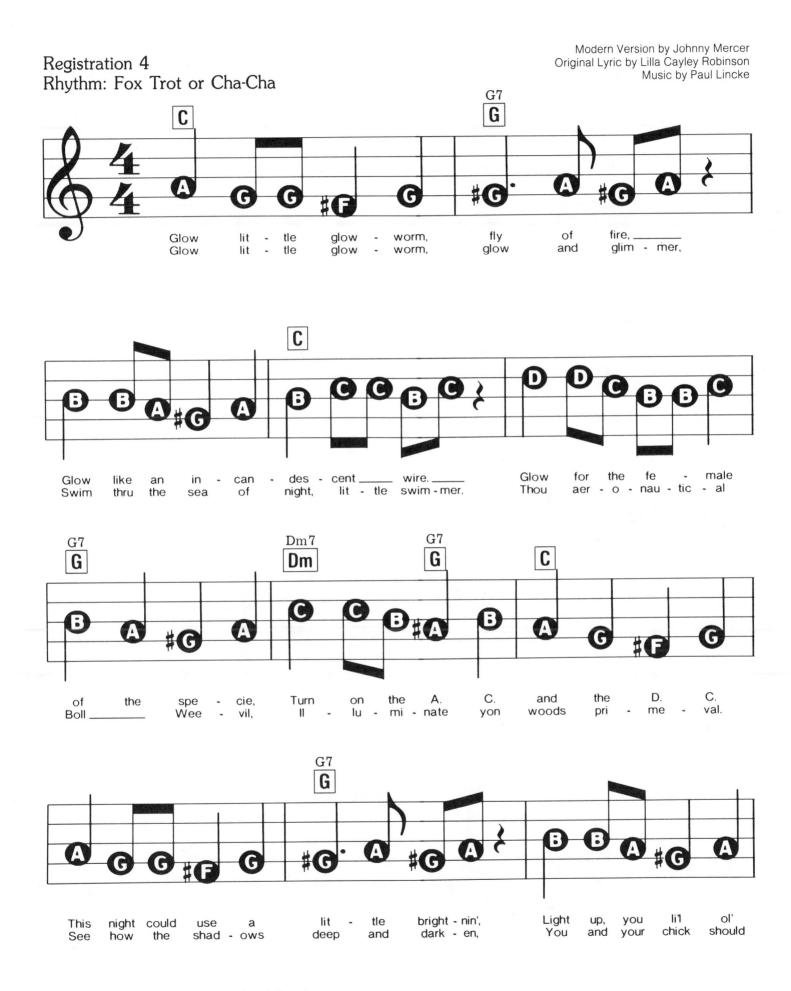

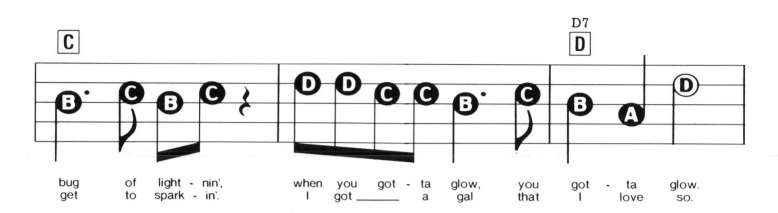

bug of light - nin',
get to spark - in'.
when you got - ta glow, you got - ta glow.
I got _____ a gal that I love so.

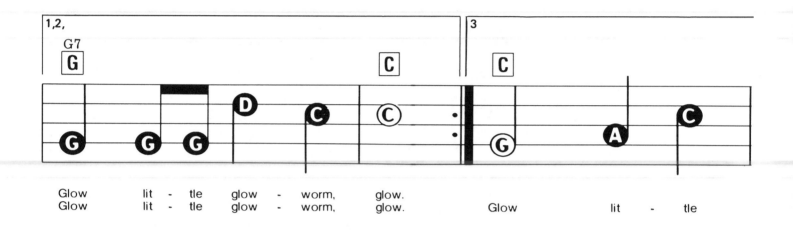

Glow lit - tle glow - worm, glow.
Glow lit - tle glow - worm, glow. Glow lit - tle

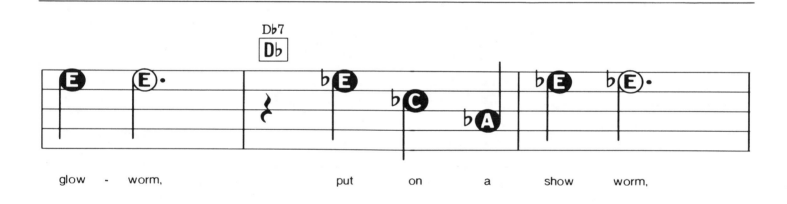

glow - worm, put on a show worm,

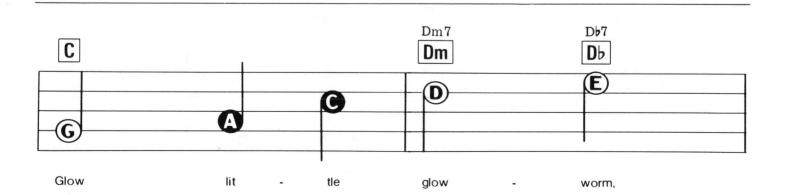

Glow lit - tle glow - worm,

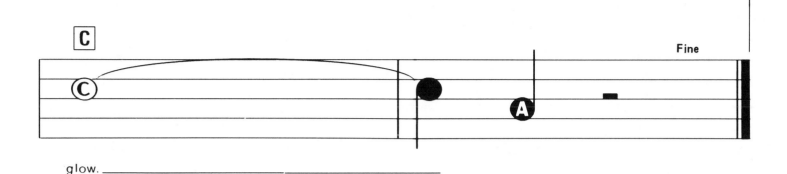

glow.

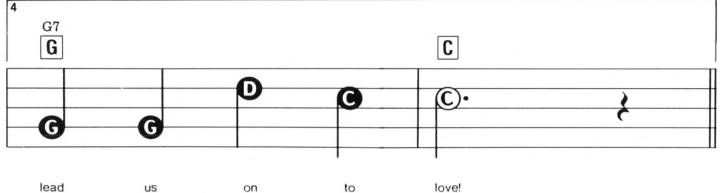

lead      us      on      to      love!

**\* Verse 3**
Glow little glowworm, turn the key on,
You are equipped with tail light neon;
You got a cute vest pocket Mazda
Which you can make both slow or "fazda;"
I don't know who you took a shine to,
Or who you're out to make a sign to.
I got a gal that I love so.
Glow little glowworm, put on a showworm,
Glow little glowworm, glow.

**\* Verse 4 (Original Verse)**
Shine little glowworm, glimmer, (glimmer)
Shine little glowworm, glimmer! (glimmer!)
Lead us lest too far we wander,
Love's sweet voice is calling yonder!
Shine little glowworm glimmer, (glimmer)
Shine little glowworm glimmer! (glimmer!)
Light the path, below, above,
And lead us to Love!

\*If Verse 3 is sung, play the 3rd ending to Fine
 If Verse 4 is sung, skip the 3rd ending and play
 the 4th ending

# Bye, Bye Love

Registration 4
Rhythm: Fox Trot or Swing

Words and Music by
Felice Bryant and Boudleaux Bryant

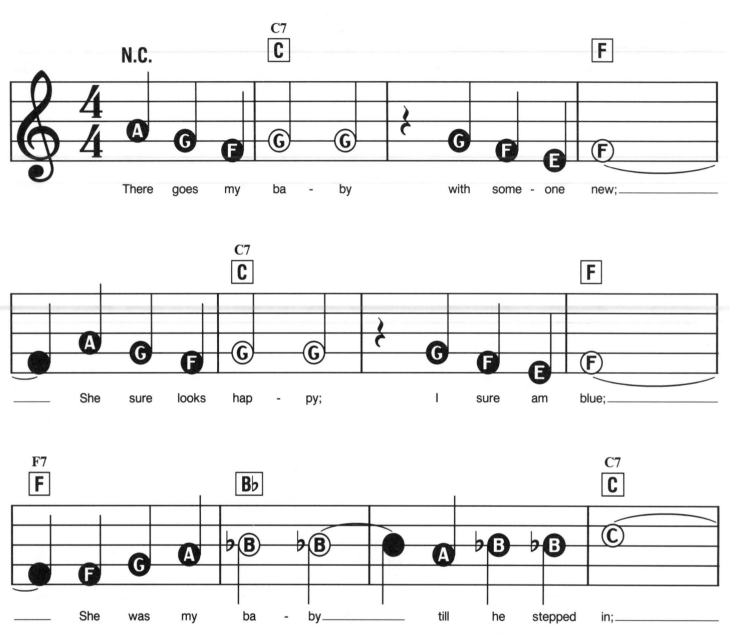

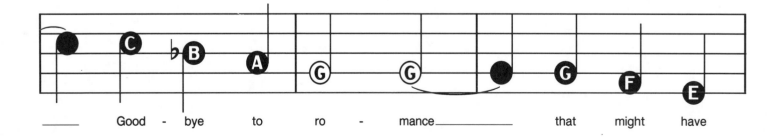

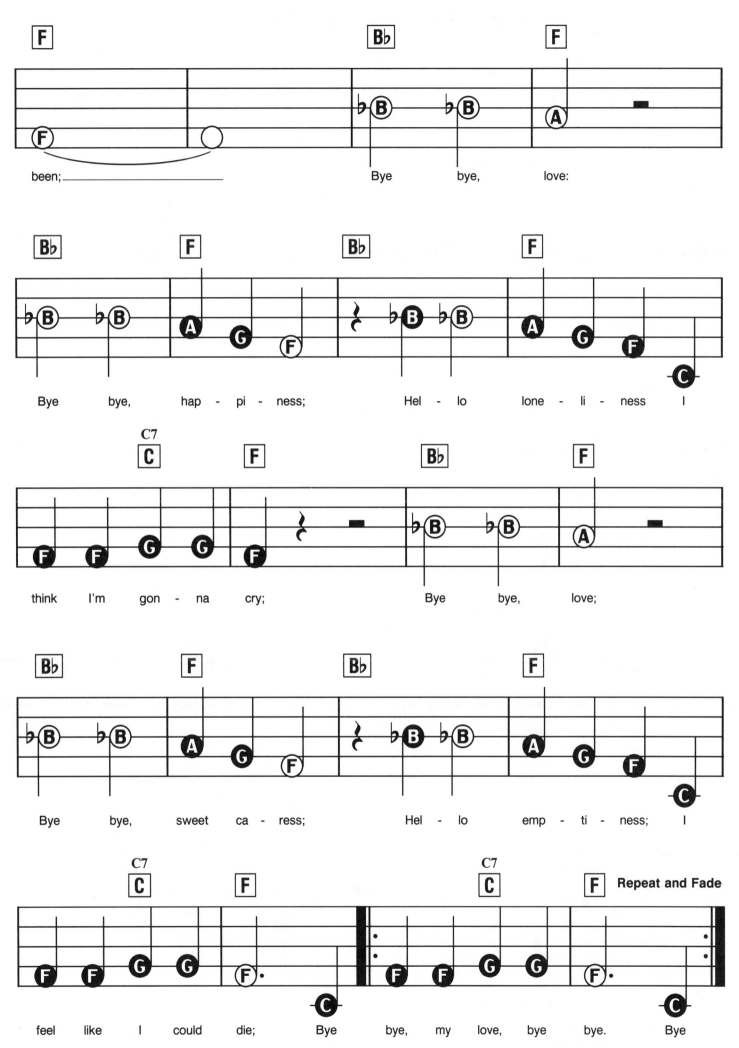

# Canadian Sunset

Registration 2
Rhythm: Fox Trot or Swing

Music by Eddie Heywood
Lyrics by Norman Gimbel

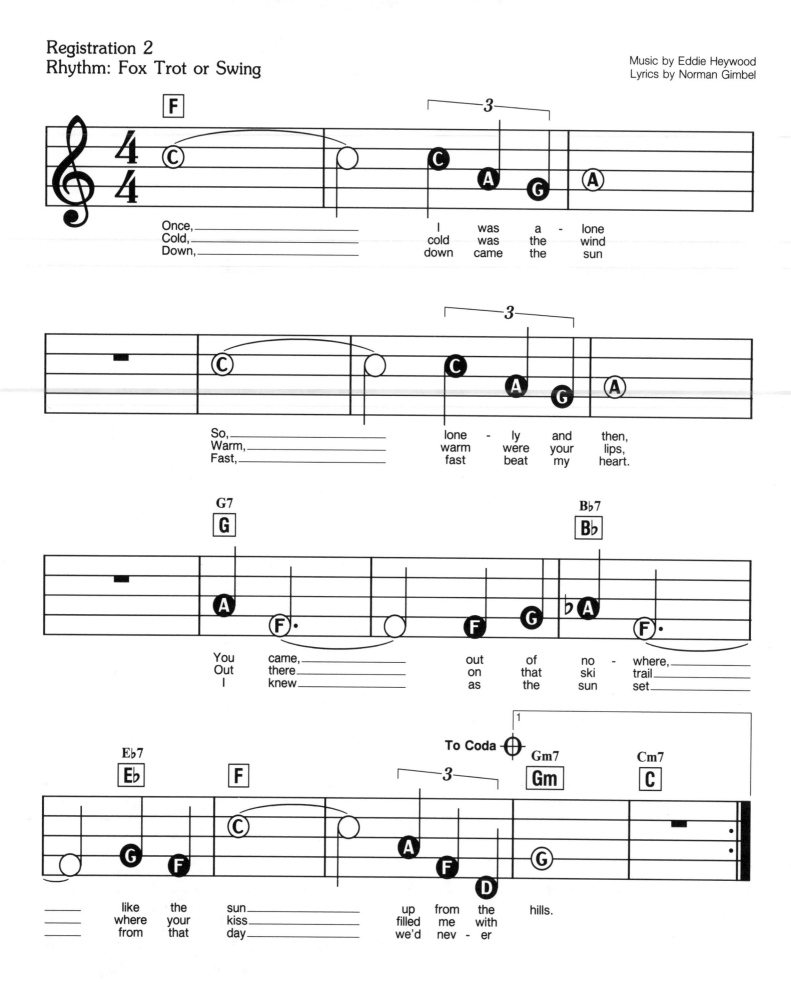

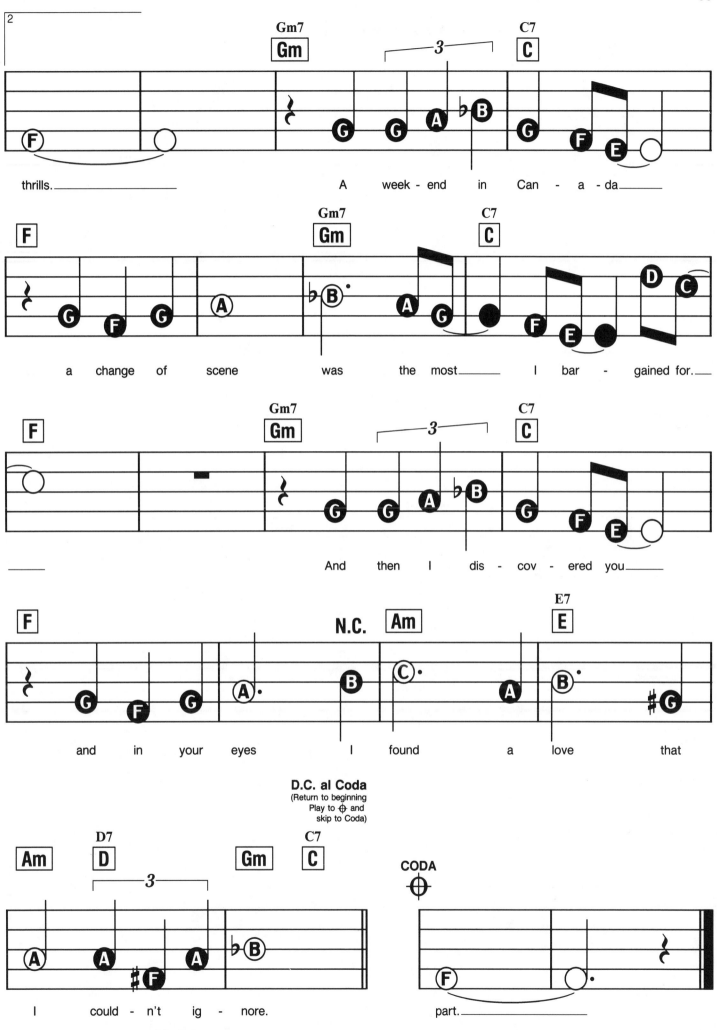

# Cara Mia

Registration 3
Rhythm: Waltz

By Tulio Trapani and Lee Lange

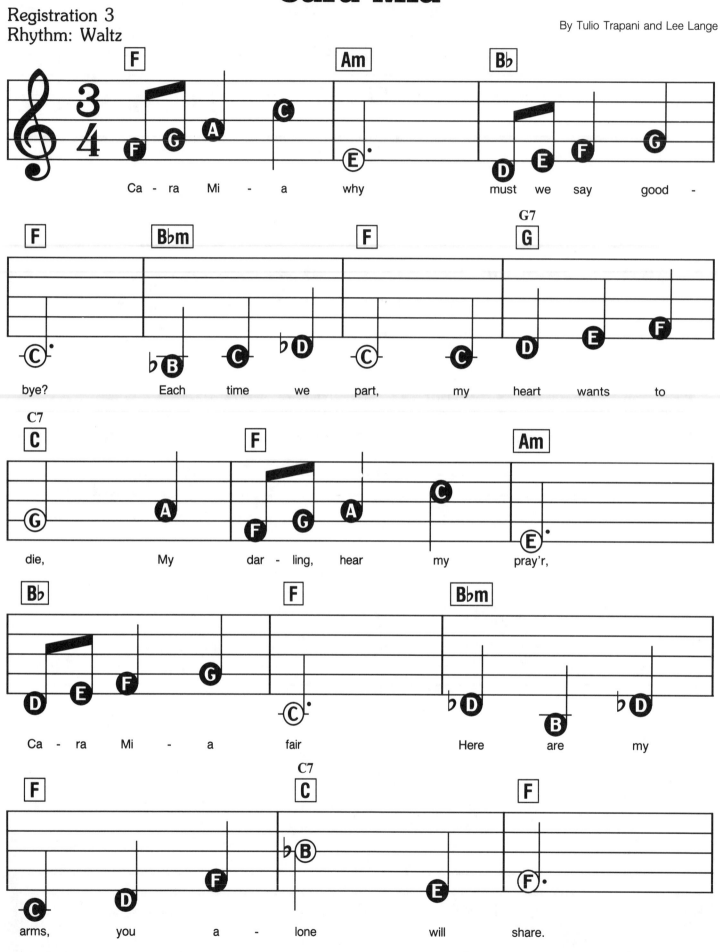

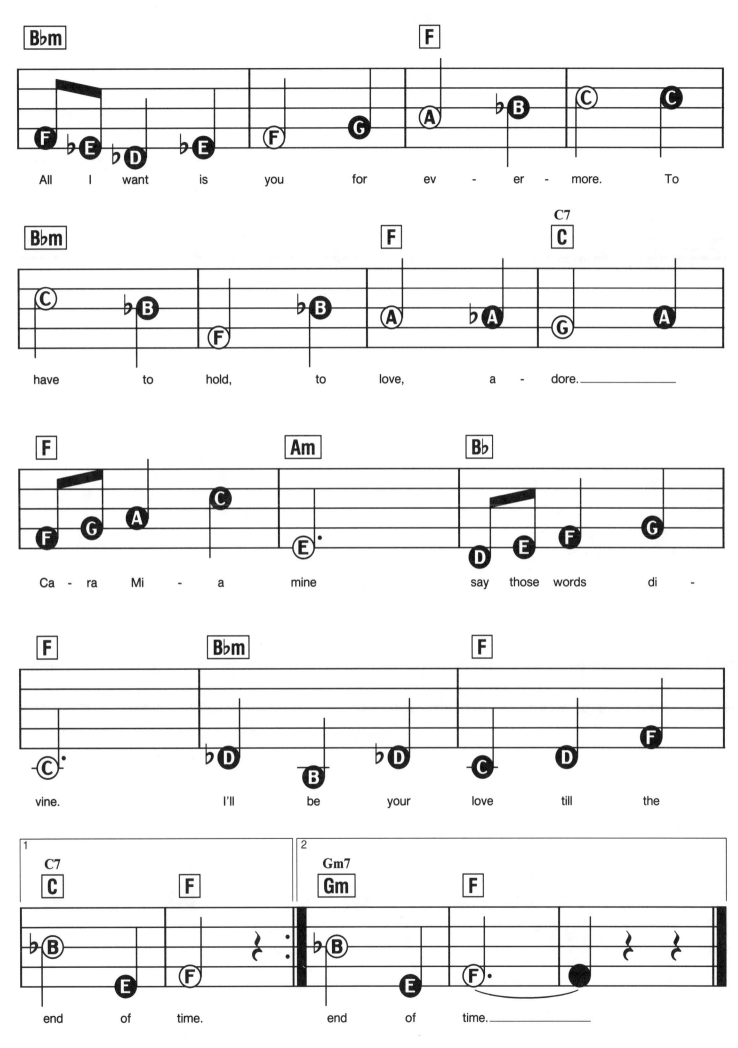

# C'est Si Bon

## (It's So Good)

Registration 2
Rhythm: Fox Trot or Swing

English Words by Jerry Seelen
French Words by Andre Hornez
Music by Henri Betti

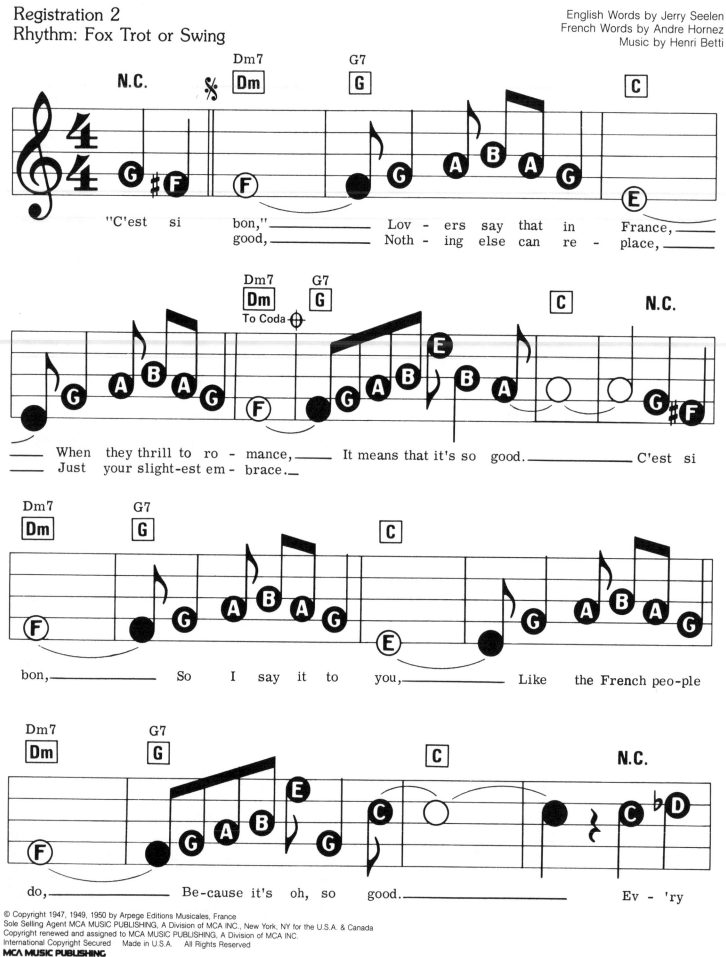

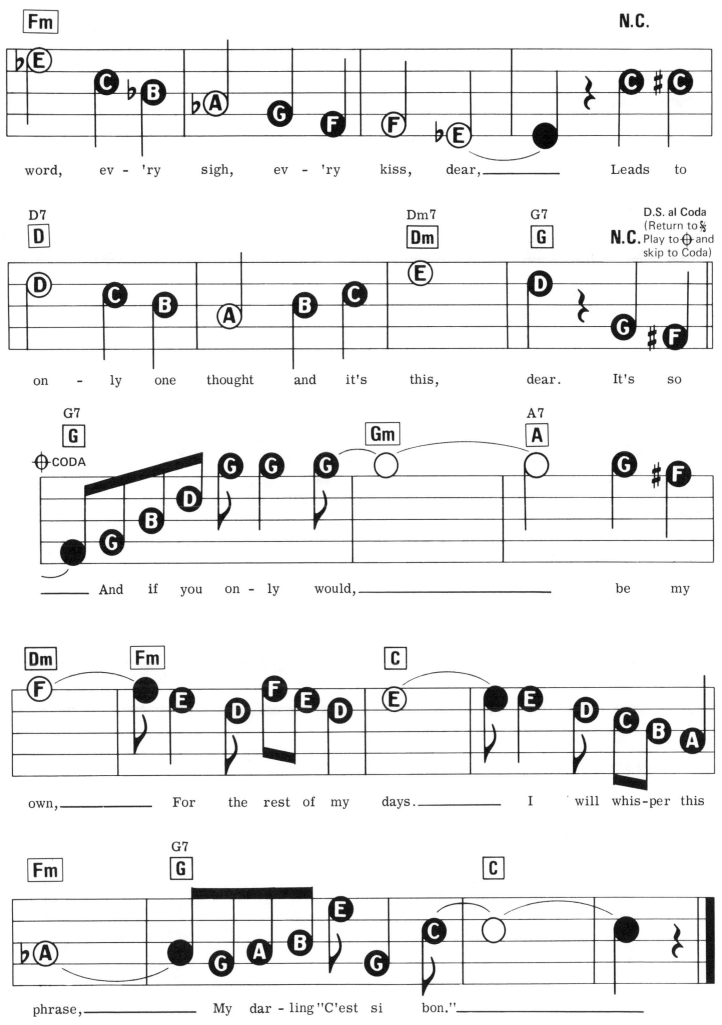

# Cherry Pink And Apple Blossom White

Registration 9
Rhythm: Latin or Rhumba

French Words by Jacques Larue
English Words by Mack David
Music by Louiguy

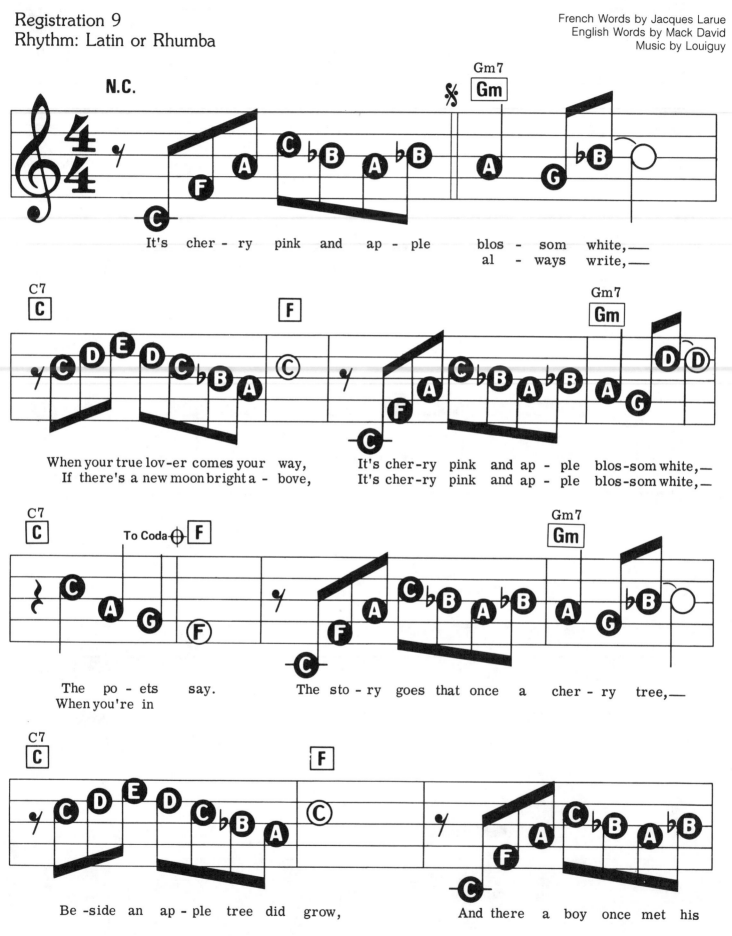

It's cher - ry pink and ap - ple blos - som white,—
al - ways write,—

When your true lov-er comes your way,
It's cher-ry pink and ap - ple blos-som white,—
If there's a new moon bright a - bove,
It's cher-ry pink and ap - ple blos-som white,—

The po - ets say.
The sto - ry goes that once a cher - ry tree,—
When you're in

Be -side an ap - ple tree did grow,
And there a boy once met his

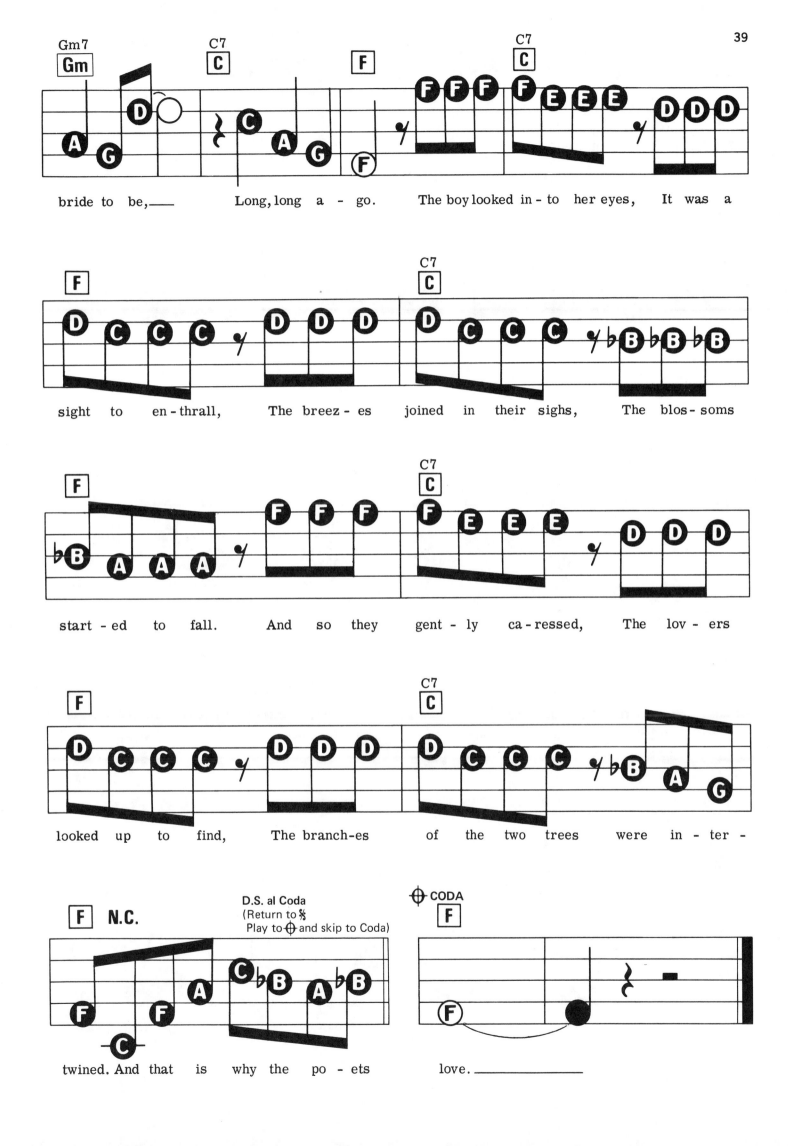

# Climb Ev'ry Mountain

(From "THE SOUND OF MUSIC")

Registration 5
Rhythm: Fox Trot or Swing

Words by Oscar Hammerstein II
Music by Richard Rodgers

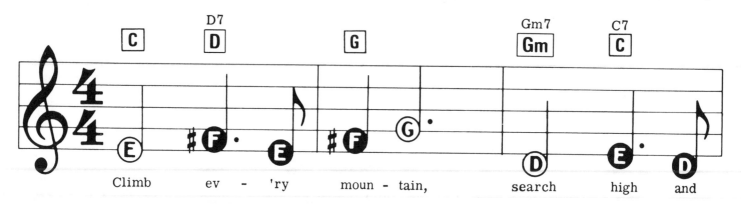

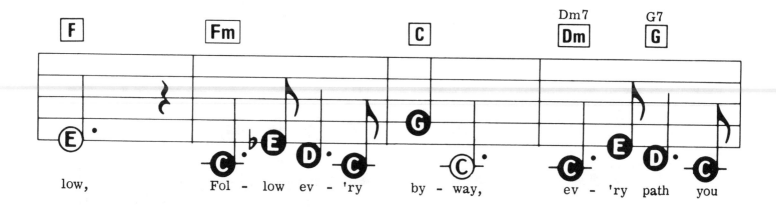

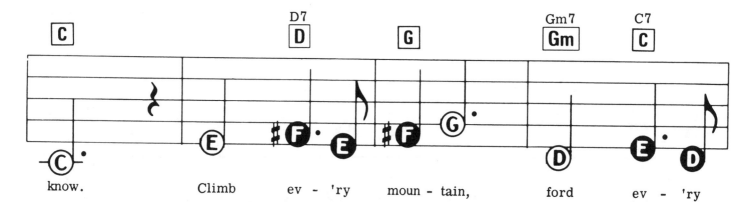

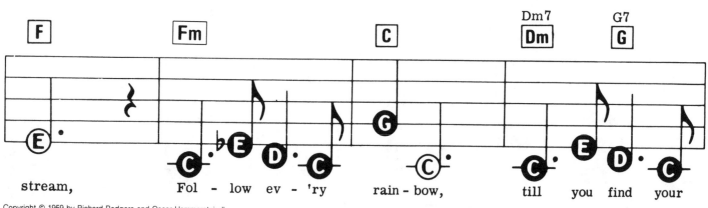

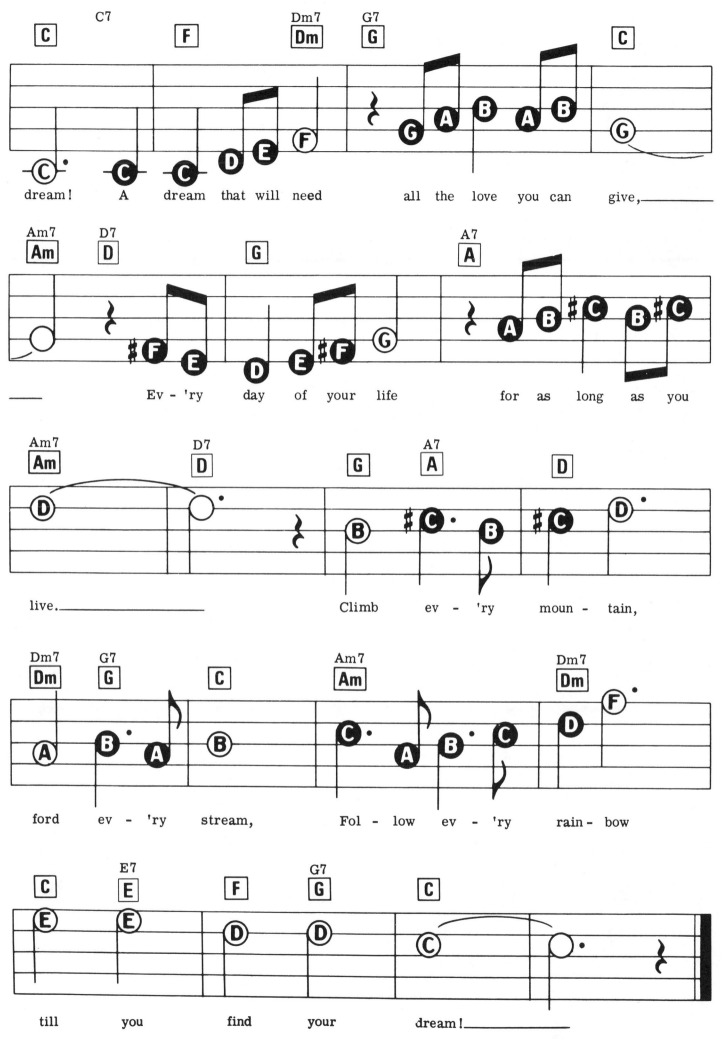

# Cry

Registration 1
Rhythm: Swing

By Churchill Kohlman

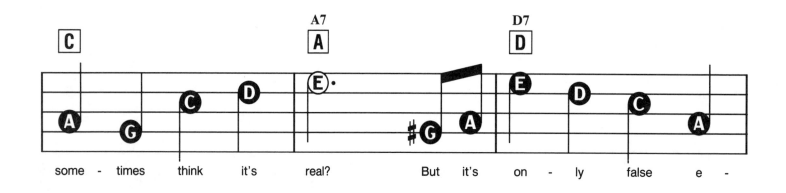

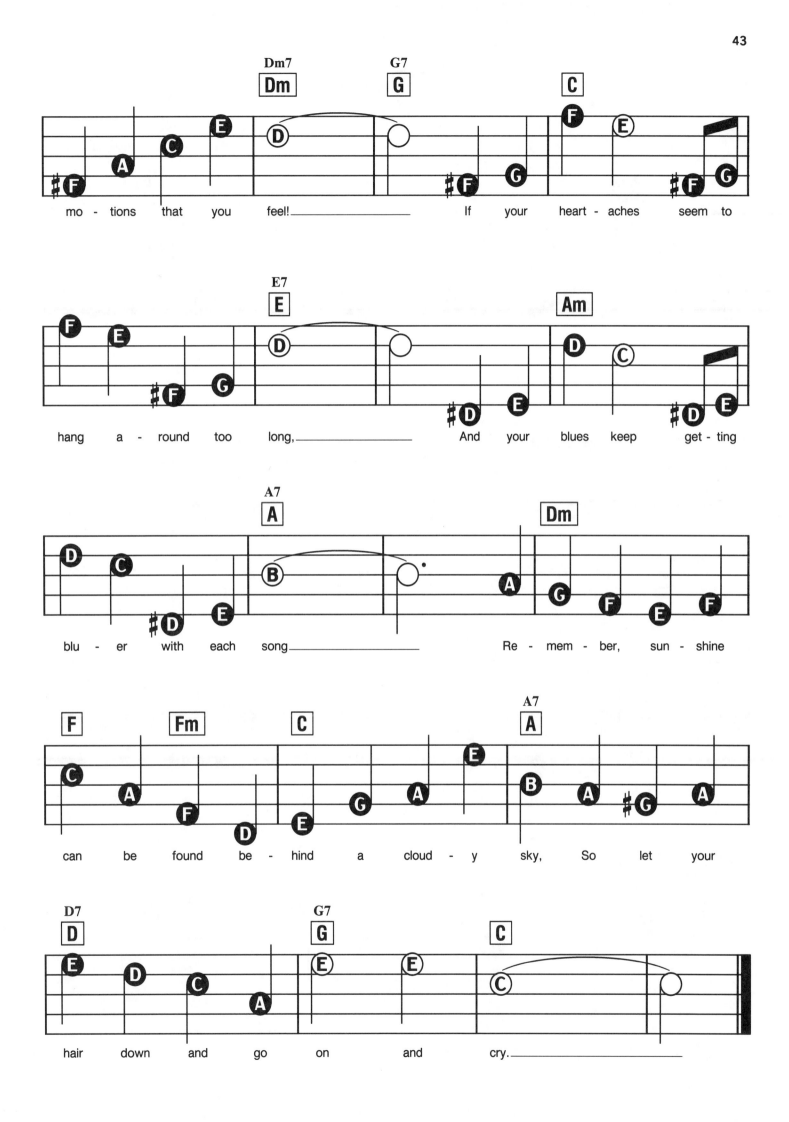

# Cry Me A River

Registration 2
Rhythm: Rox Trot

Words and Music by
Arthur Hamilton

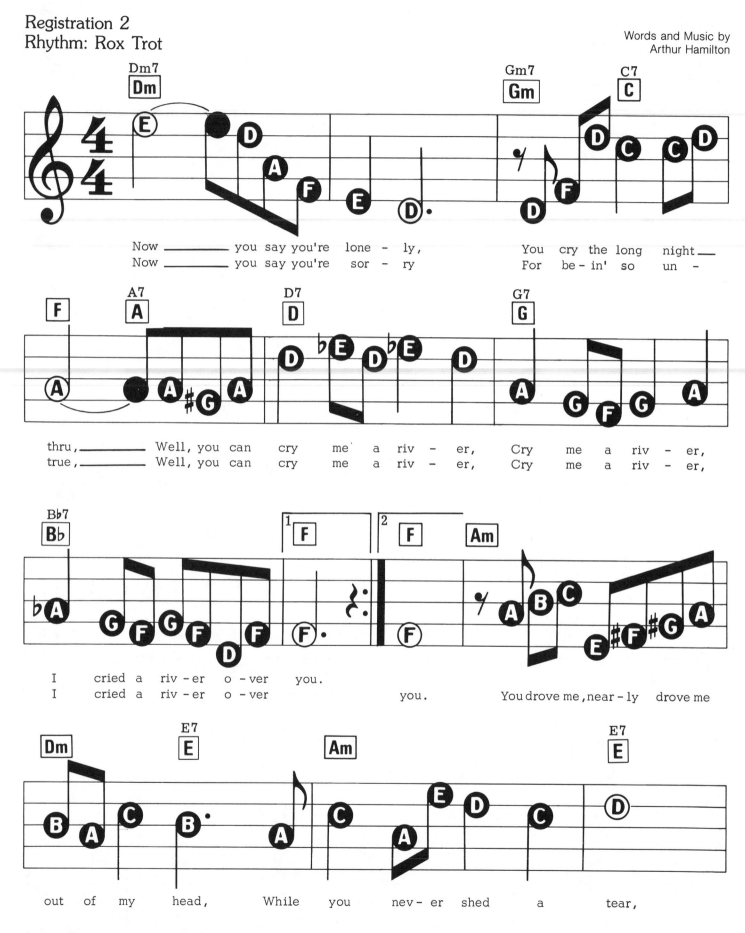

Now _____ you say you're lone - ly,    You    cry the long    night ___
Now _____ you say you're sor - ry    For   be - in' so un -

thru, _____ Well, you can    cry    me  a  riv - er,    Cry    me  a  riv - er,
true, _____ Well, you can    cry    me  a  riv - er,    Cry    me  a  riv - er,

I    cried a  riv - er  o - ver    you.
I    cried a  riv - er  o - ver         you.    You drove me, near - ly  drove me

out  of  my  head,    While    you    nev - er  shed  a    tear,

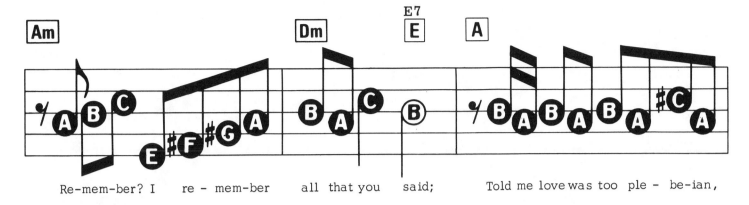

Re-mem-ber? I re - mem-ber all that you said; Told me love was too ple - be-ian,

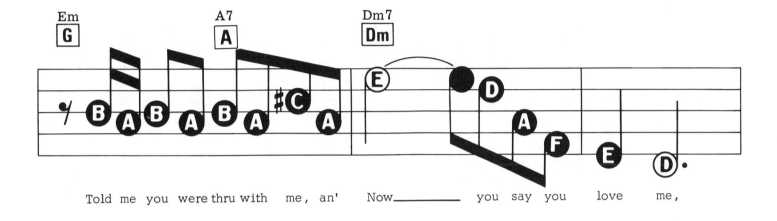

Told me you were thru with me, an' Now_____ you say you love me,

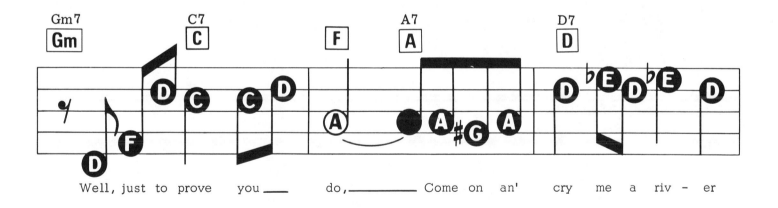

Well, just to prove you ___ do,_____ Come on an' cry me a riv - er

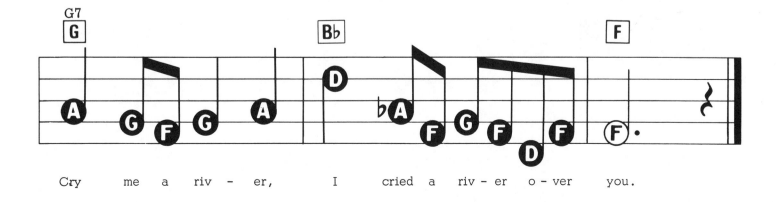

Cry me a riv - er, I cried a riv - er o - ver you.

# Crying In The Chapel

Registration 2
Rhythm: Swing

Words and Music by
Artie Glenn

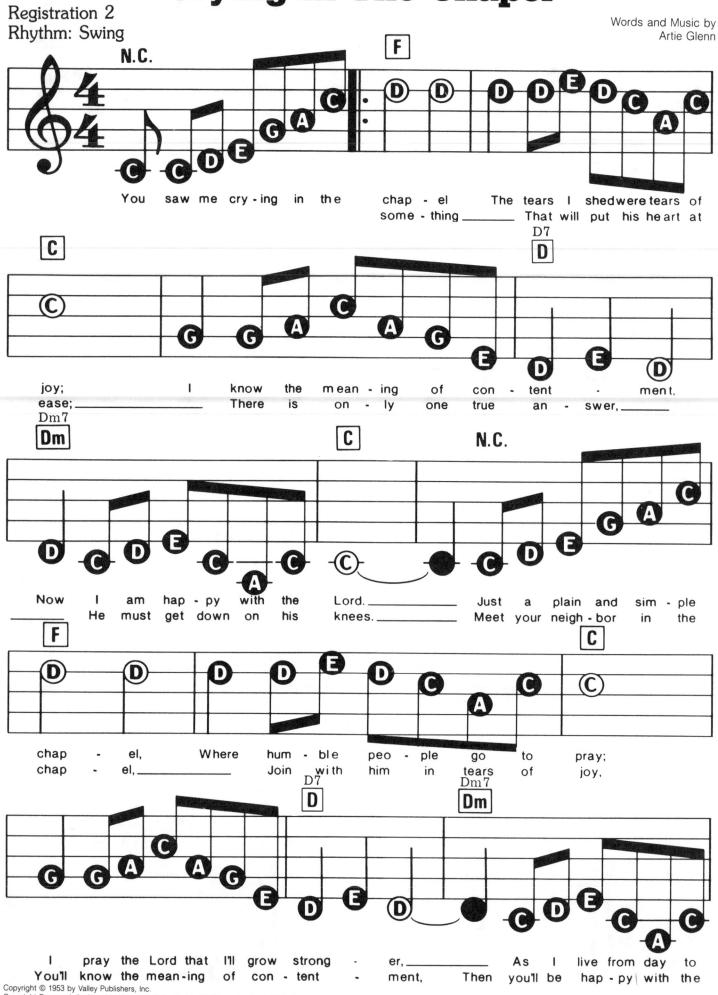

# Don't Be Cruel
## (To A Heart That's True)

Registration 4
Rhythm: Rock

Words and Music by
Otis Blackwell and Elvis Presley

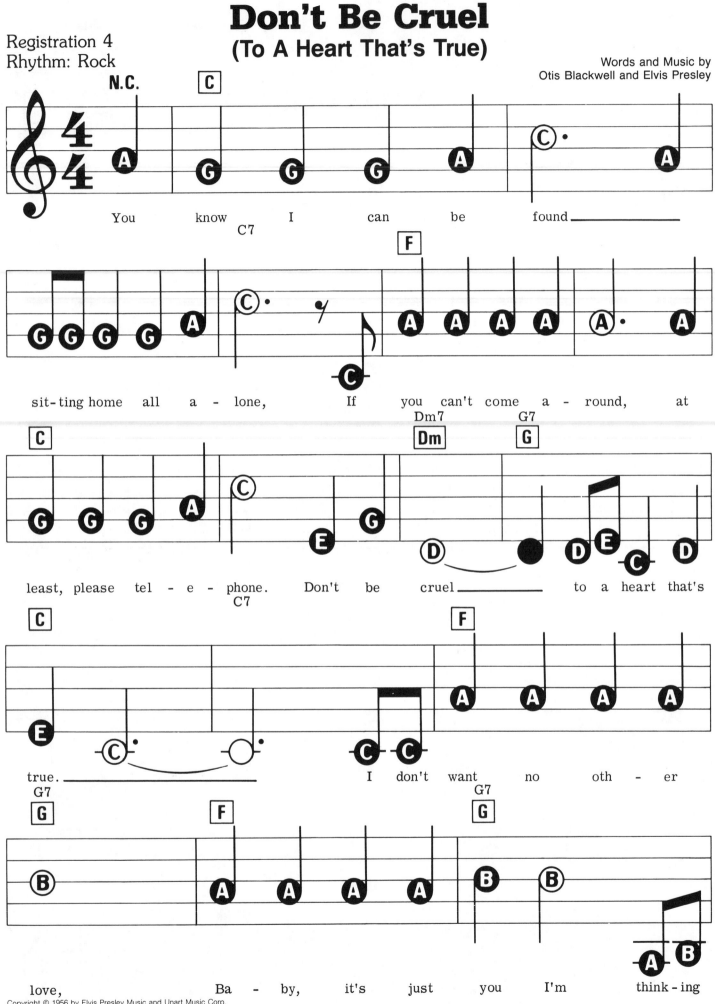

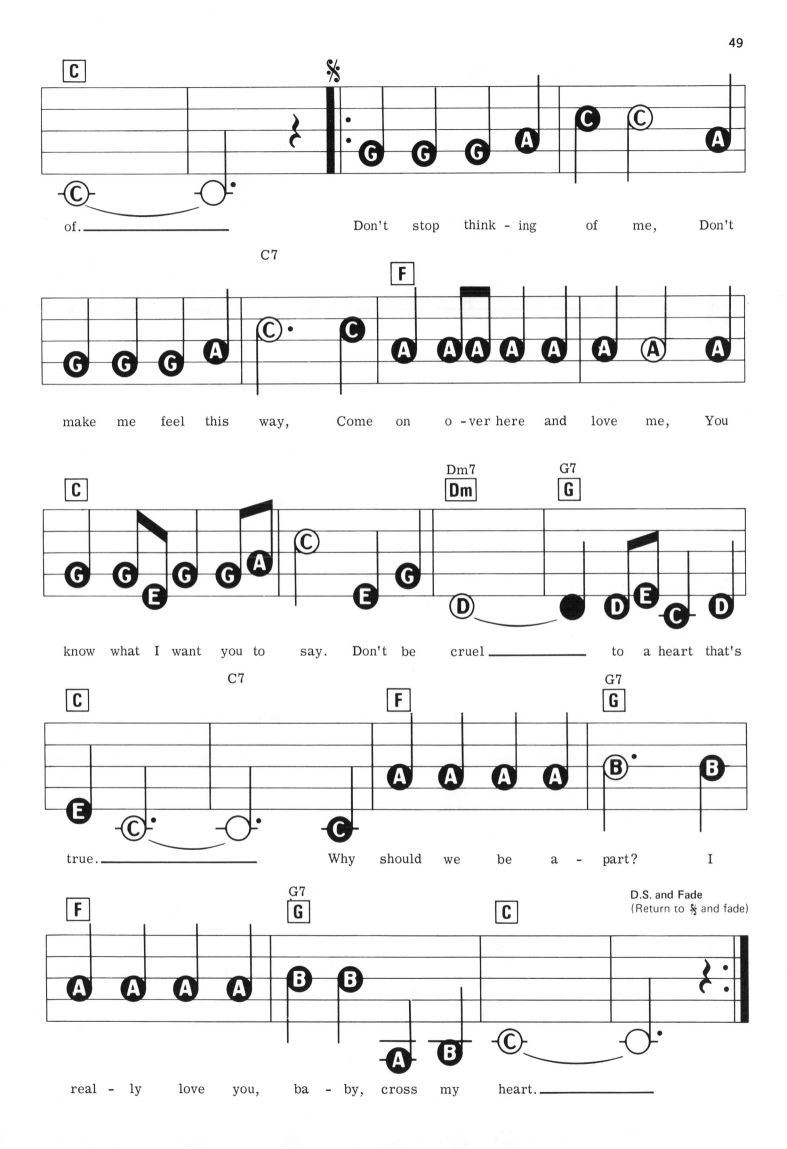

# Everything's Coming Up Roses

(From "GYPSY")

Registration 1
Rhythm: Fox Trot or Polka

Words by Stephen Sondheim
Music by Jule Styne

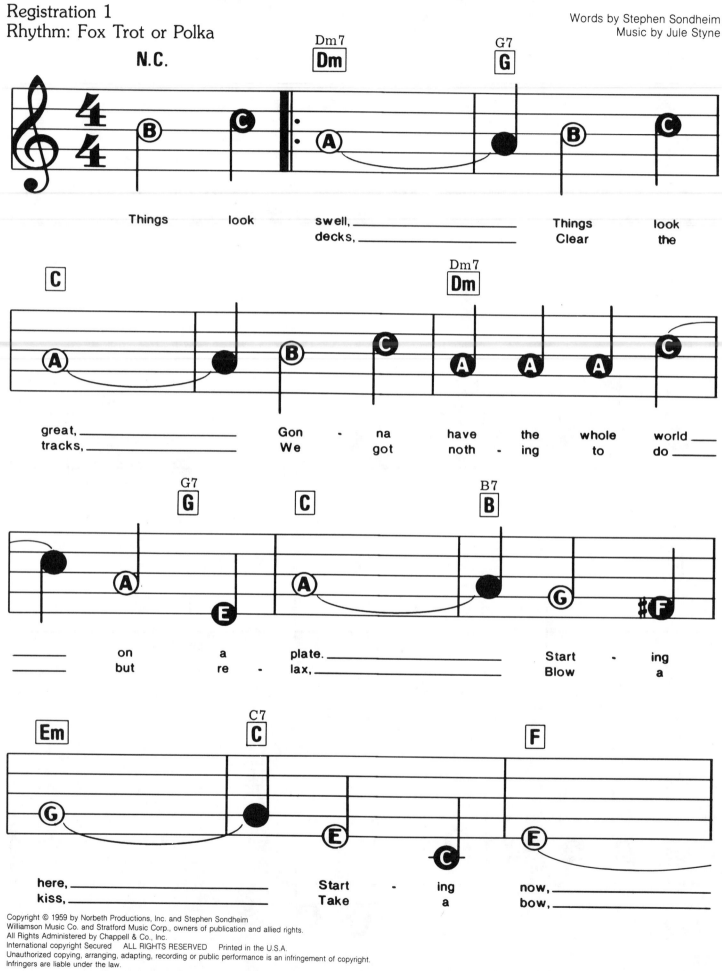

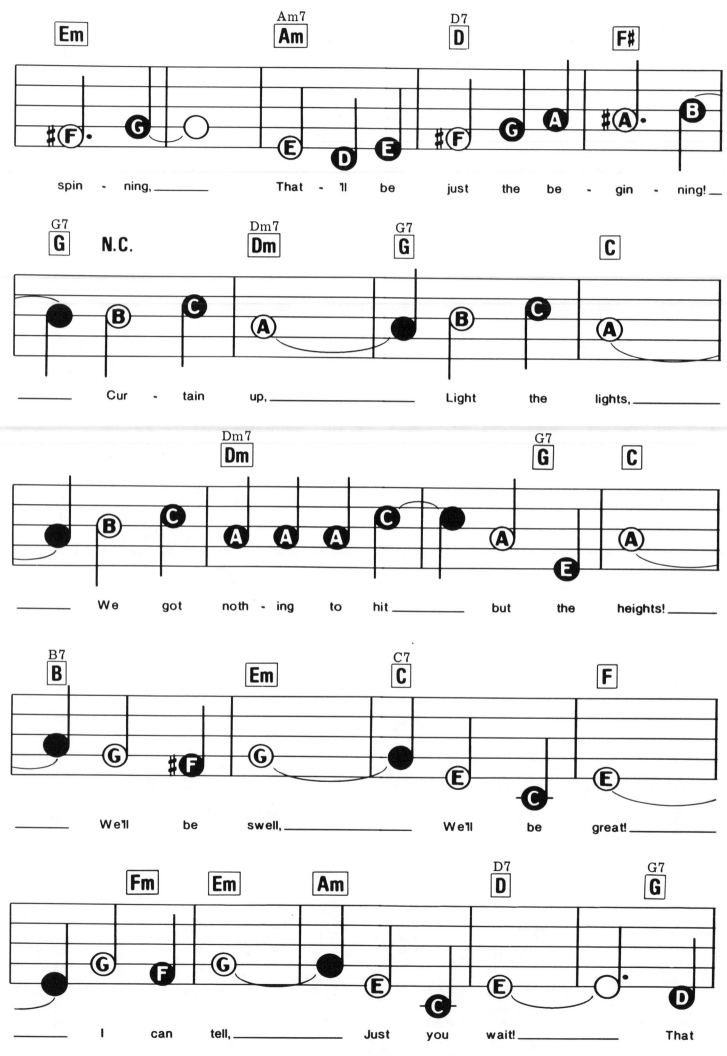

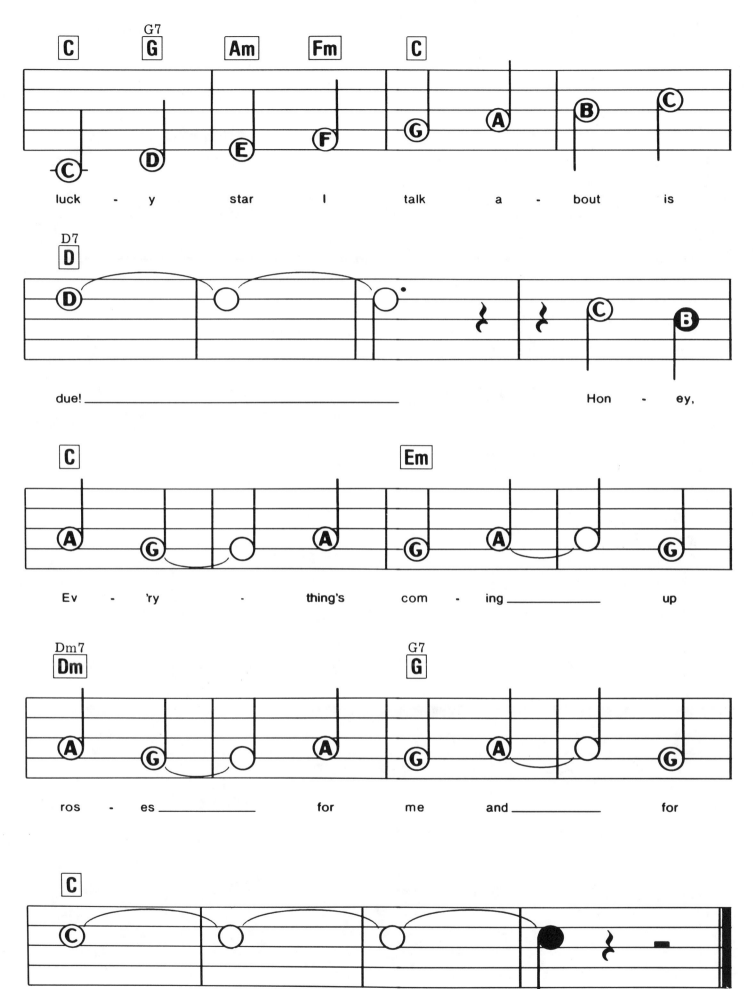

luck - y star I talk a - bout is

due! _____ Hon - ey,

Ev - 'ry - thing's com - ing _____ up

ros - es _____ for me and _____ for

you. _____

# Fever

Registration 9
Rhythm: Ballad

Words and Music by
John Davenport and Eddie Cooley

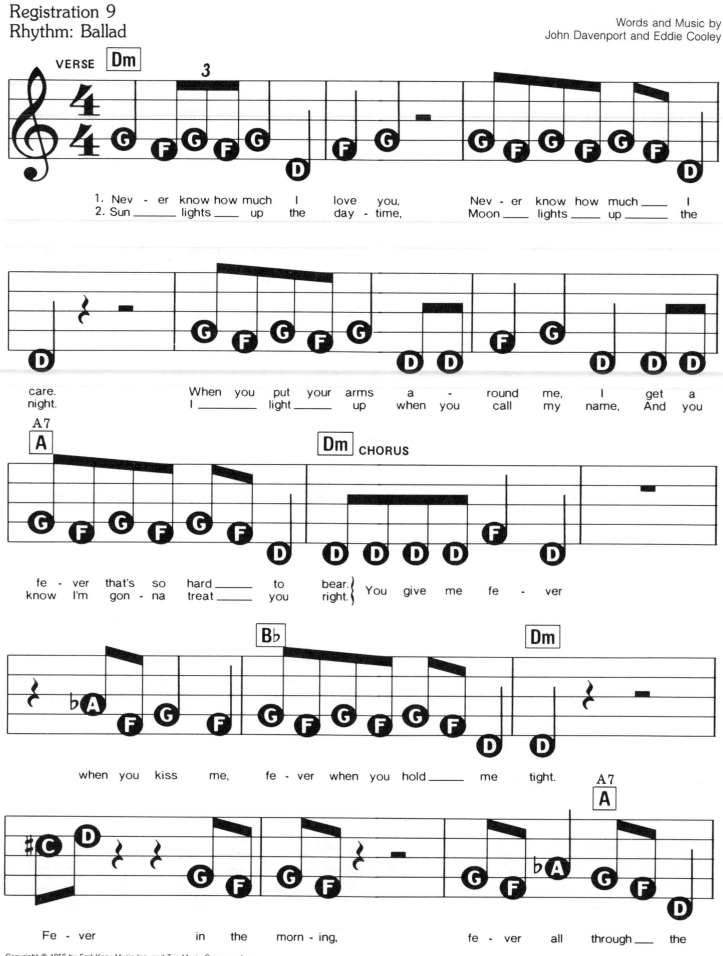

1. Nev - er know how much I love you, Nev - er know how much I
2. Sun lights up the day - time, Moon lights up the

care. When you put your arms a - round me, I get a
night. I light up when you call my name, And you

fe - ver that's so hard to bear. } You give me fe - ver
know I'm gon - na treat you right. }

when you kiss me, fe - ver when you hold me tight.

Fe - ver in the morn - ing, fe - ver all through the

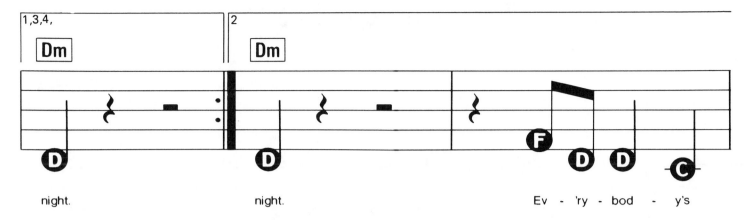

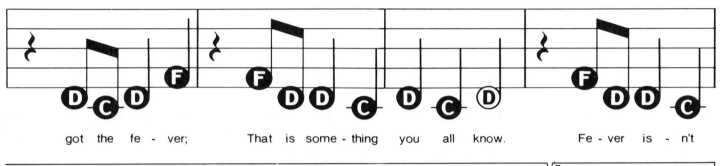

got the fe - ver; That is some - thing you all know. Fe - ver is - n't

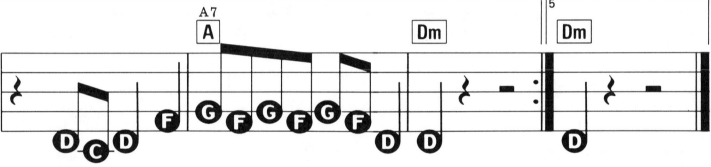

such a new thing, Fe - ver start - ed long _____ a - go. burn.

**Additional Verses**

**Verse 3**
Romeo loved Juliet,
Juliet she felt the same.
When he put his arms around her, he said,
"Julie, baby, you're my flame."

**Chorus:**
Thou givest fever, when we kisseth,
FEVER with thy flaming youth.
FEVER — I'm afire,
FEVER, yea I burn forsooth.

**Verse 4**
Captain Smith and Pocahantas
Had a very mad affair,
When her Daddy tried to kill him, she said,
"Daddy-o don't you dare."

**Chorus:**
Give me fever, with his kisses,
FEVER when he holds me tight.
FEVER — I'm his Missus,
Oh Daddy won't you treat him right.

**Verse 5**
Now you've listened to my story
Here's the point that I have made.
Chicks were born to give you FEVER
Be it fahrenheit or centigrade.

**Chorus:**
They give you FEVER, when you kiss them,
FEVER if you live and learn.
FEVER — till you sizzle,
What a lovely way to burn.

# The Green Door

Registration 5
Rhythm: Rock

Words and Music by
Bob Davie and Marvin Moore

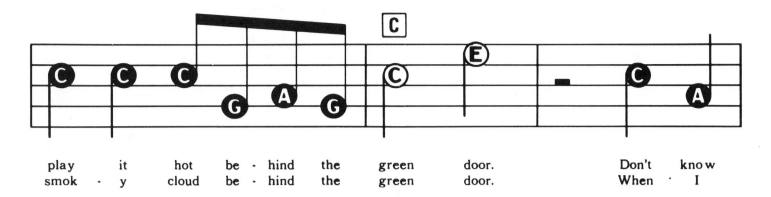

play    it    hot    be - hind    the    green    door.    Don't    know
smok - y    cloud    be - hind    the    green    door.    When    I

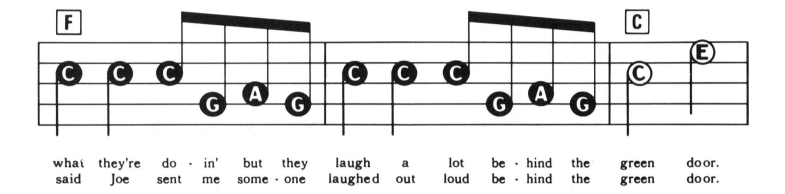

what    they're    do - in'    but    they    laugh    a    lot    be - hind    the    green    door.
said    Joe    sent    me    some - one    laughed    out    loud    be - hind    the    green    door.

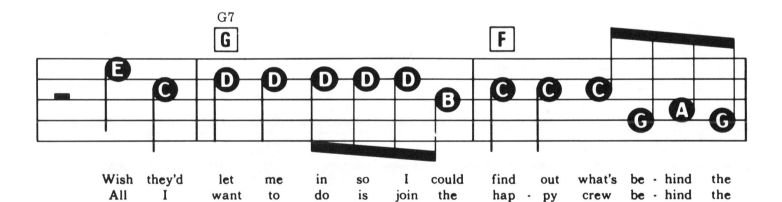

Wish    they'd    let    me    in    so    I    could    find    out    what's    be - hind    the
All    I    want    to    do    is    join    the    hap - py    crew    be - hind    the

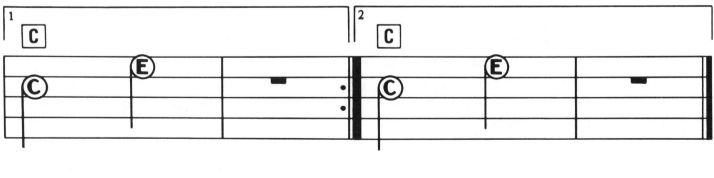

green    door.    green    door.

# Heartbreak Hotel

Registration 3
Rhythm: Ballad

By Mae Boren Axton, Tommy Durden
and Elvis Presley

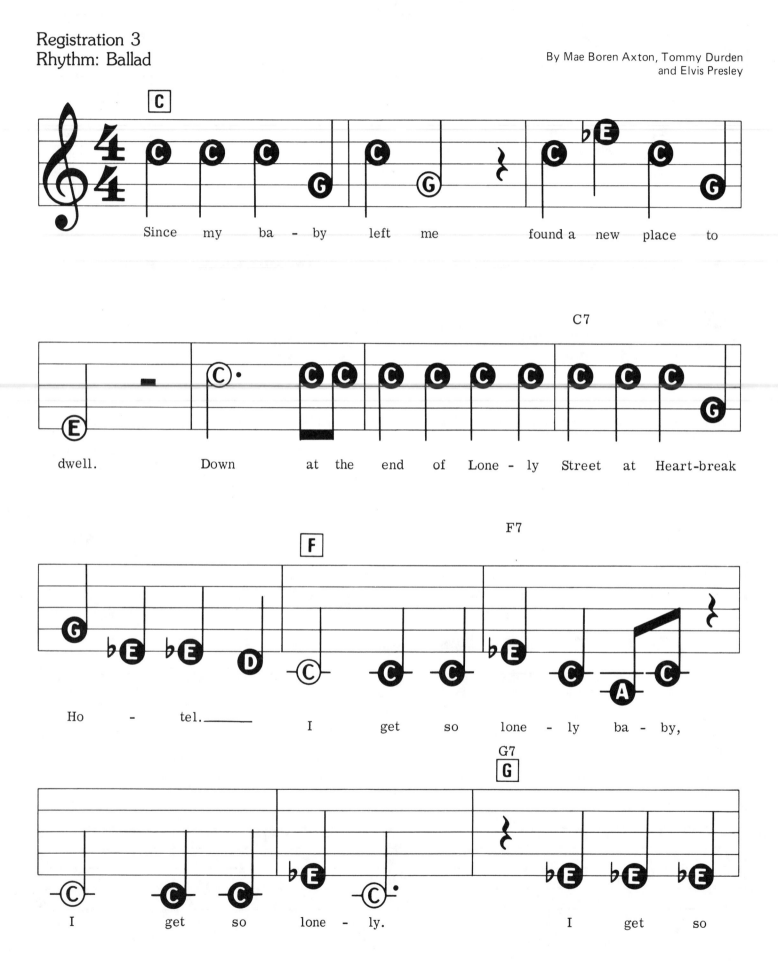

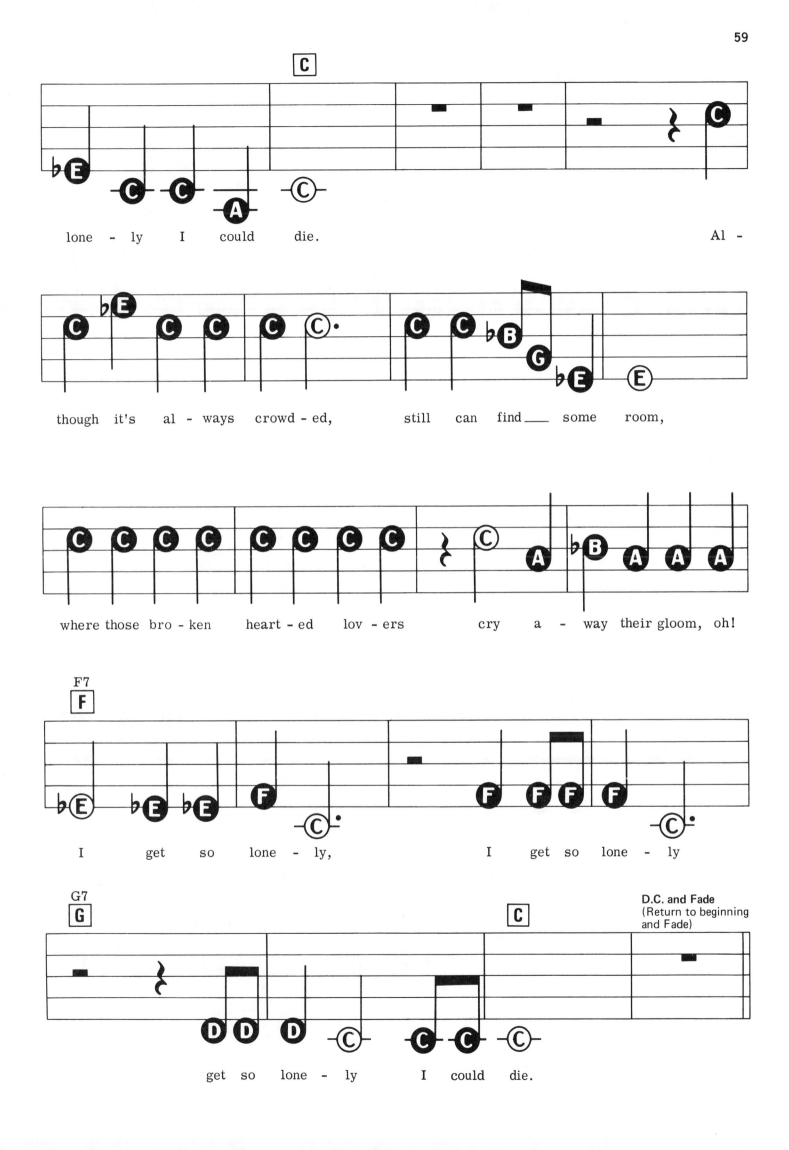

# Here's That Rainy Day

Registration 2
Rhythm: Ballad or Slow Rock

Words and Music by
Johnny Burke and James Van Heusen

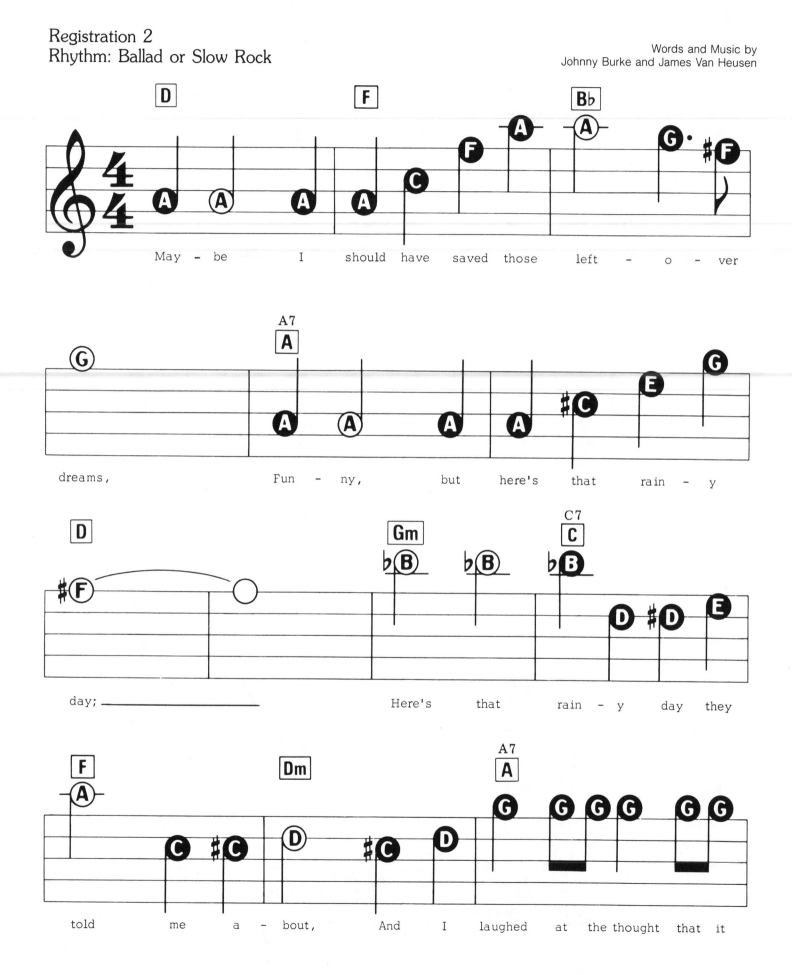

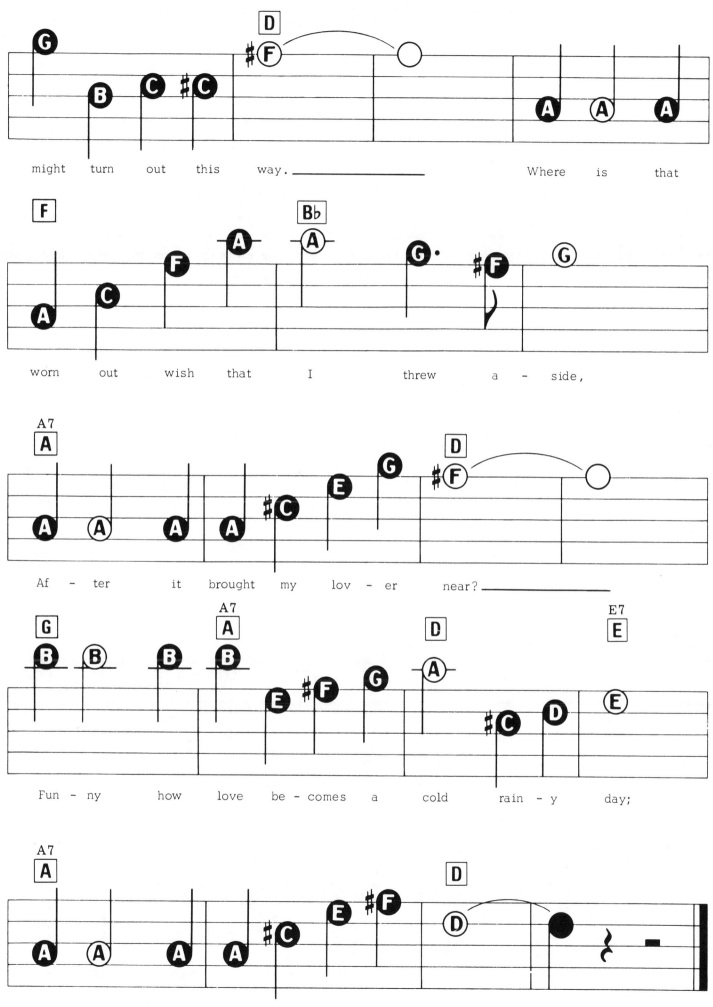

# I Believe

Registration 2
Rhythm: Ballad or Slow Rock

Words and Music by Ervin Drake,
Irvin Graham, Jimmy Shirl and Al Stillman

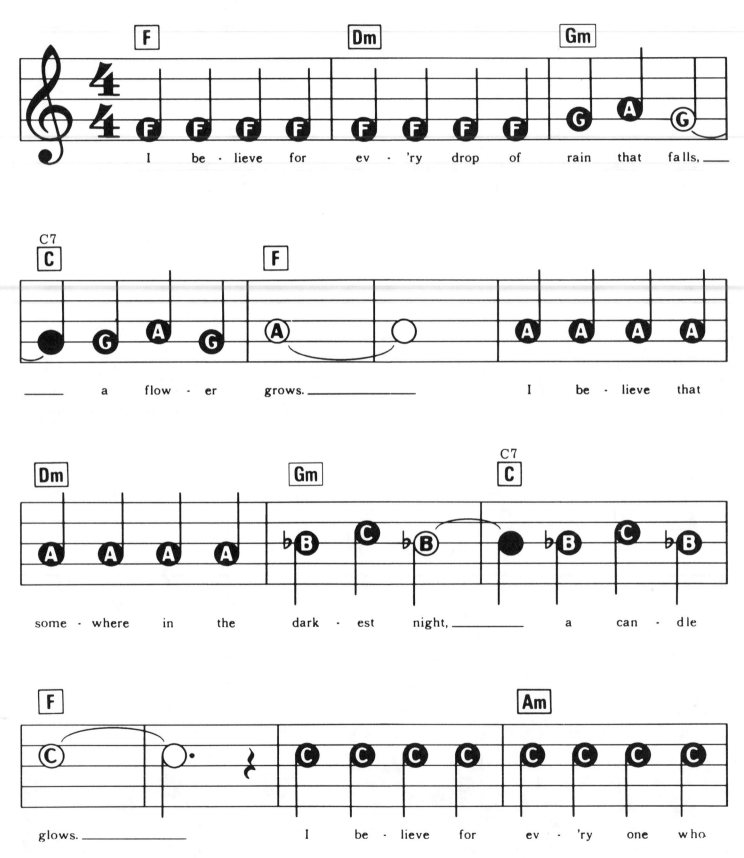

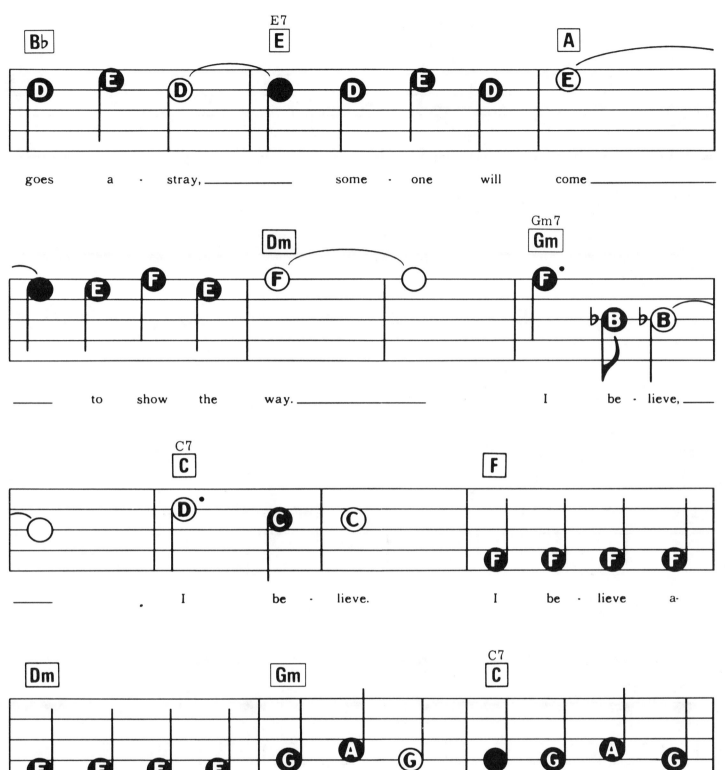

goes a - stray,_____ some - one will come _____

_____ to show the way._____ I be - lieve,_____

_____ . I be - lieve. I be - lieve a-

bove the storm the small - est pray'r _____ will still be

heard. _____ I be - lieve that some - one in the

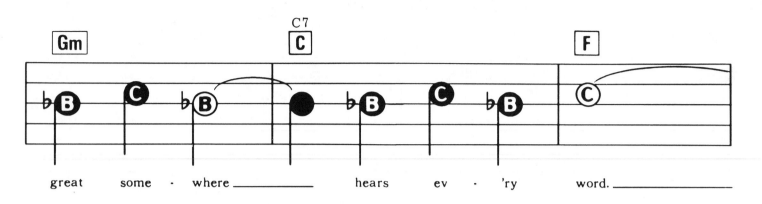

great    some - where _____ hears    ev -  'ry     word. _____

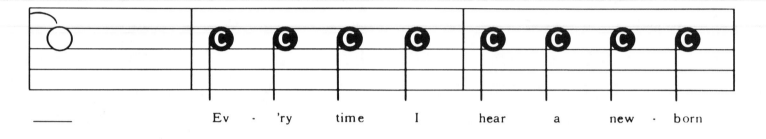

_____    Ev -  'ry    time    I    hear    a    new - born

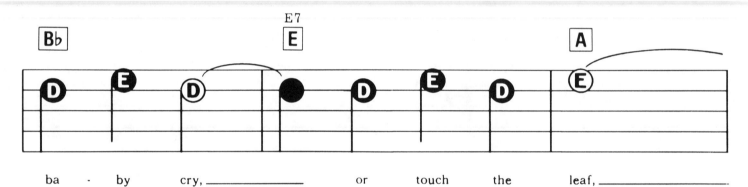

ba -   by    cry, _____    or    touch    the    leaf, _____

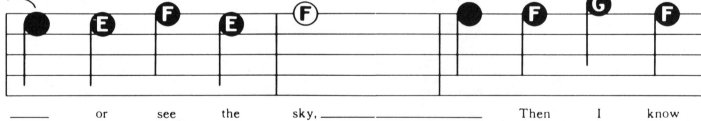

_____    or    see    the    sky, _____    Then    I    know

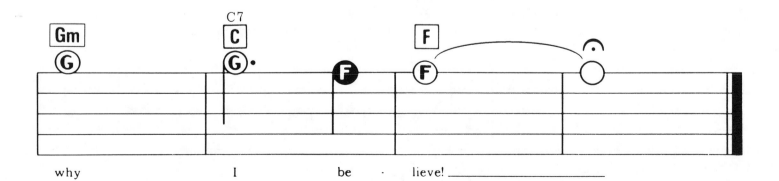

why    I    be - lieve! _____

# Mr. Wonderful
### (From The Musical "MR. WONDERFUL")

Registration 9
Rhythm: Fox Trot

Words and Music by Jerry Bock,
Larry Holofcener and George Weiss

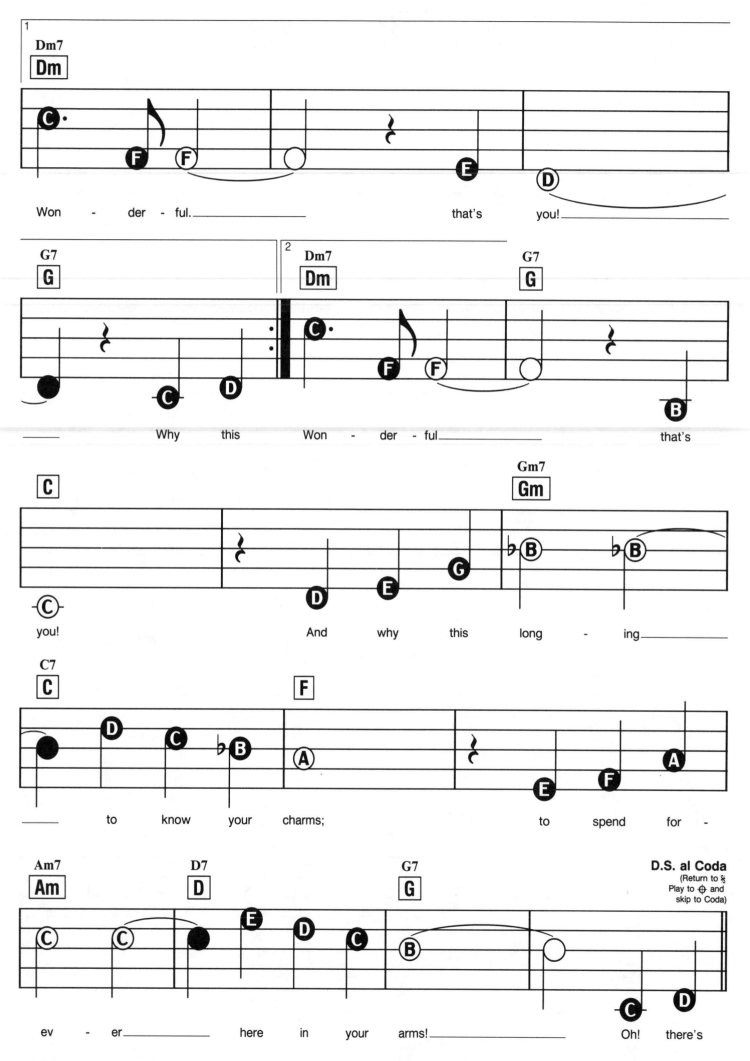

# I Love Paris

Registration 9
Rhythm: Fox Trot

Words and Music by
Cole Porter

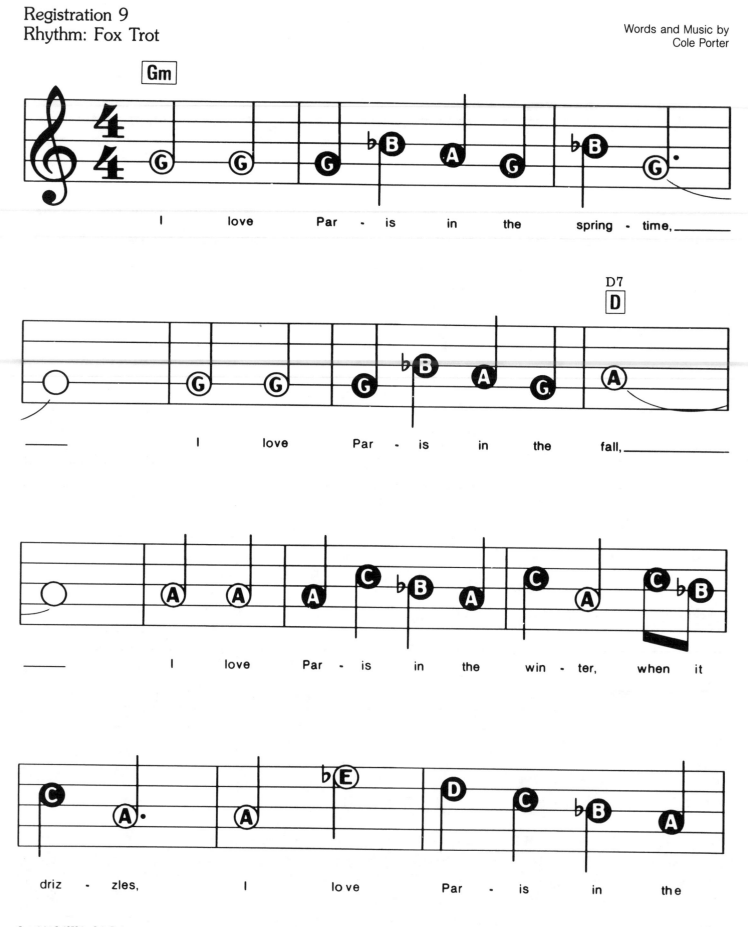

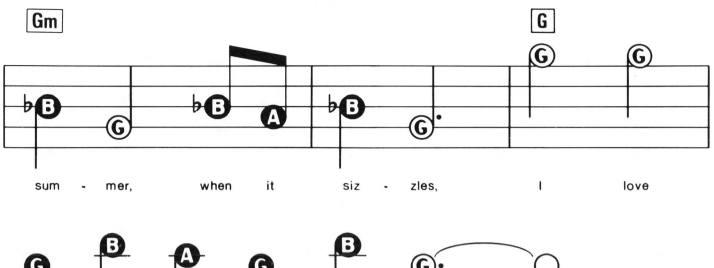

sum - mer, when it siz - zles, I love

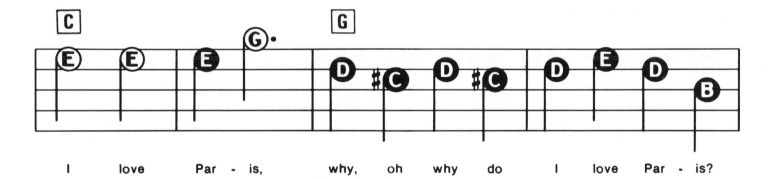

Pa - ris ev - 'ry mo - ment, _____

ev - 'ry mo - ment of the year, _____

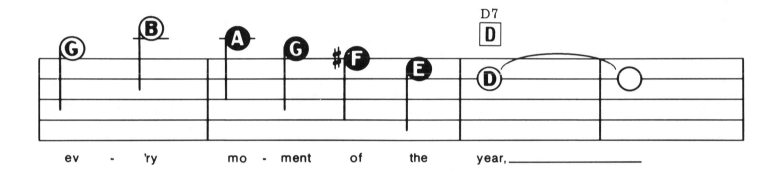

I love Par - is, why, oh why do I love Par - is?

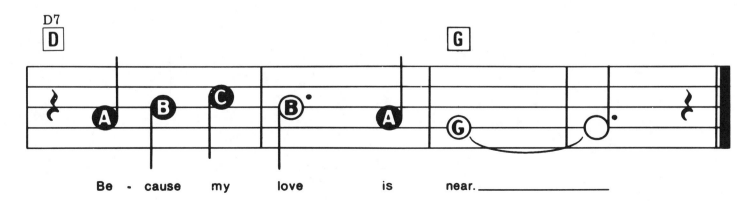

Be - cause my love is near. _____

# I Talk To The Trees
## (From "PAINT YOUR WAGON")

Registration 2
Rhythm: Slow Rock or Ballad

Words by Alan Jay Lerner
Music by Frederick Loewe

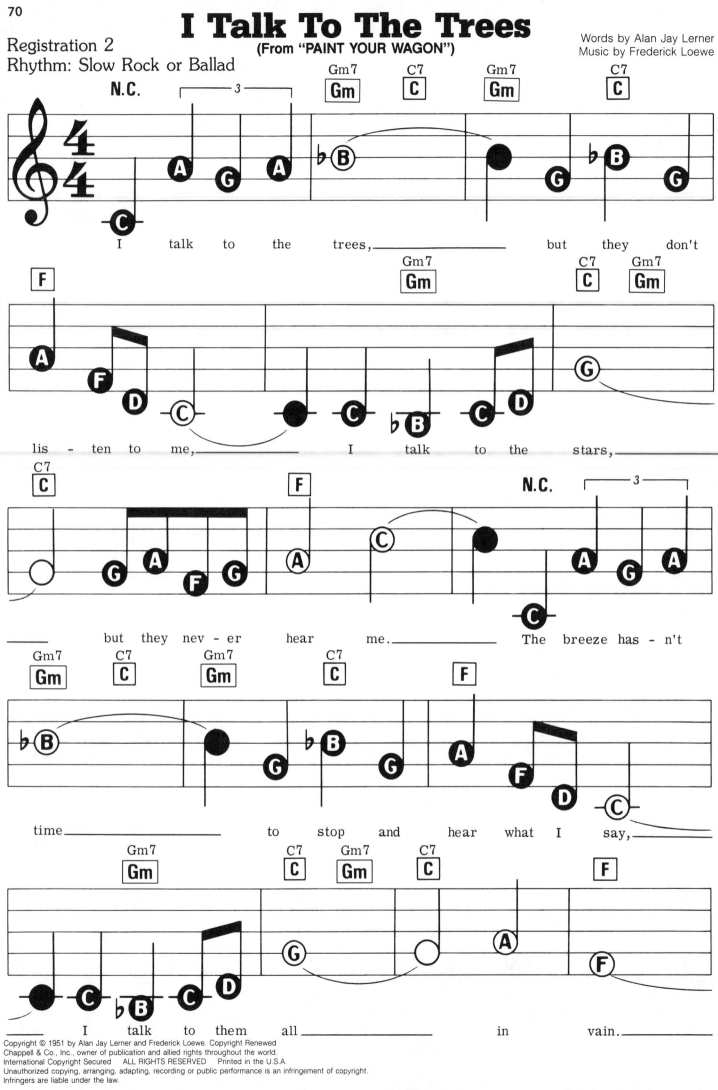

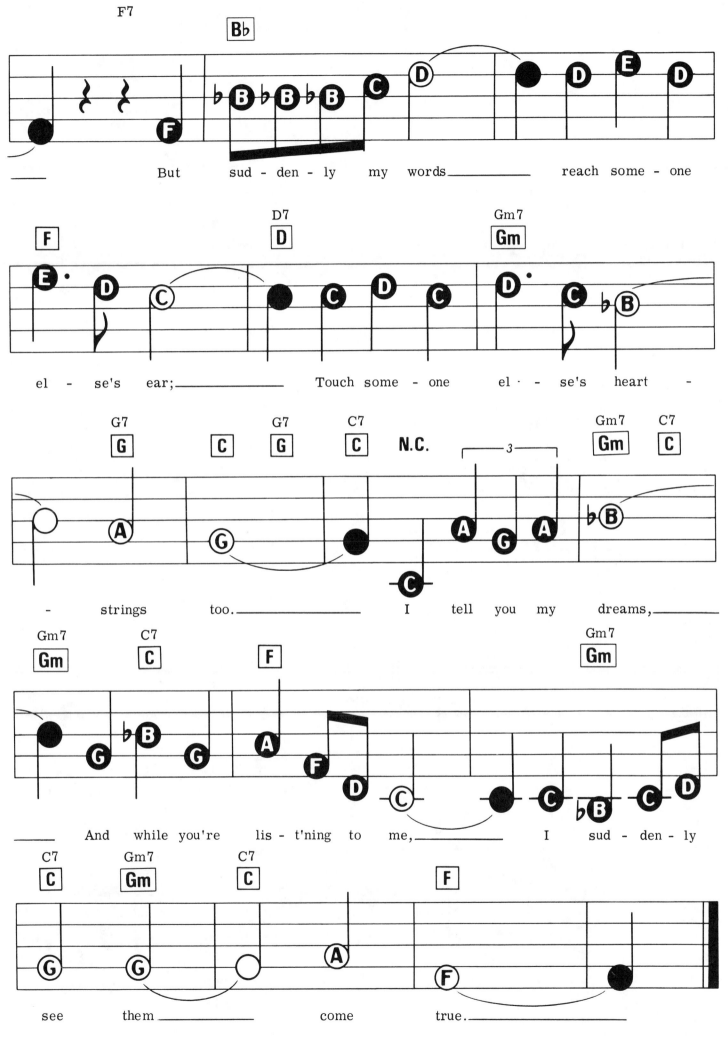

# It's All In The Game

Registration 4
Rhythm: Swing

Lyric by Carl Sigman
Music by Charles G. Dawes

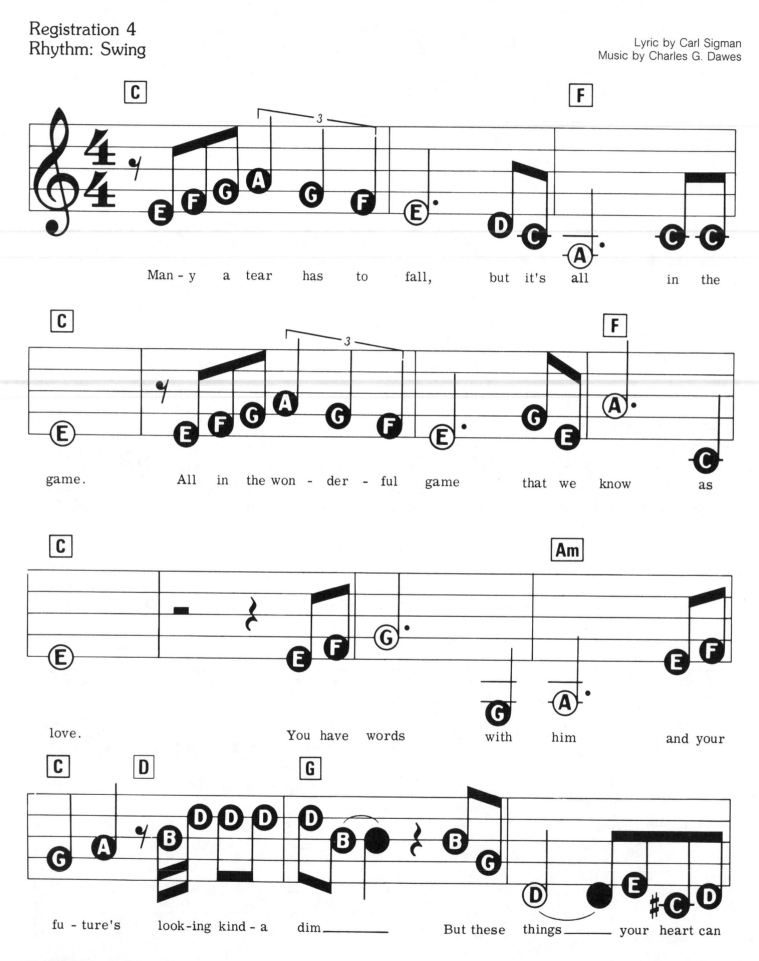

Man-y a tear has to fall, but it's all in the game. All in the won - der - ful game that we know as love. You have words with him and your fu - ture's look-ing kind - a dim But these things your heart can

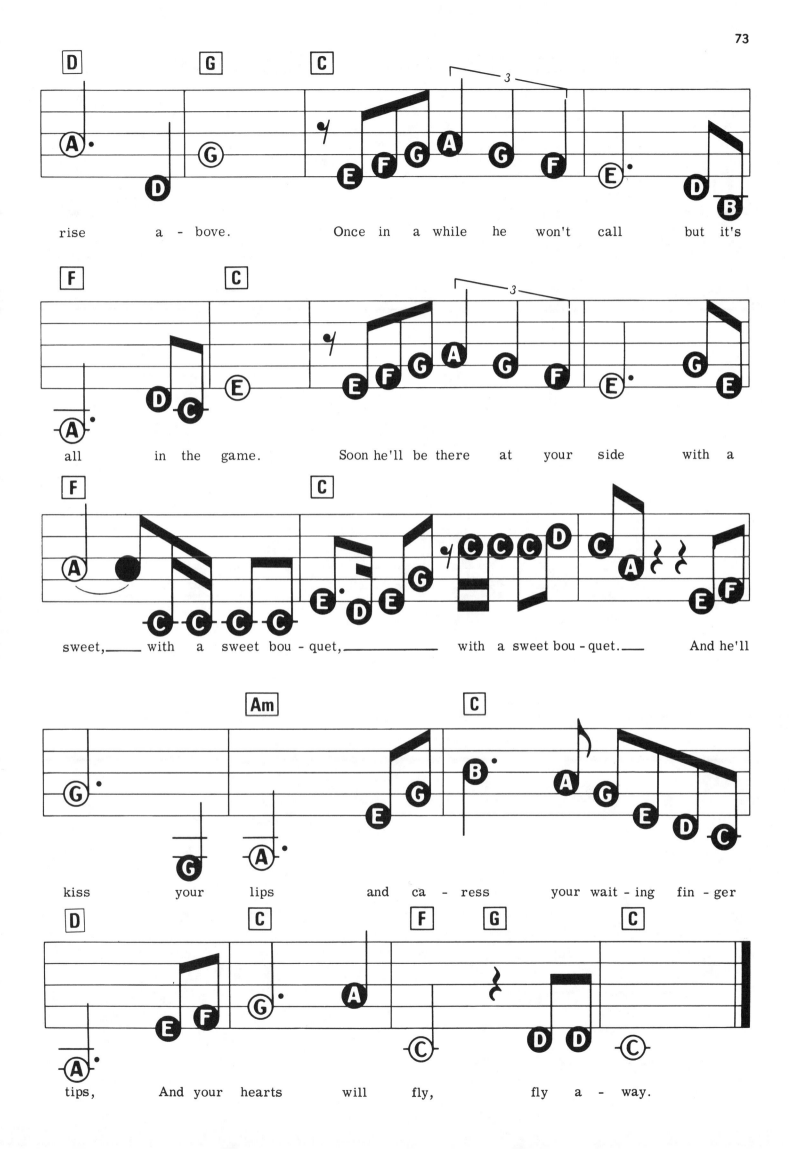

# It's Just A Matter Of Time

Registration 6
Rhythm: Country

Words and Music by Clyde Otis,
Brook Benton and Belford Hendricks

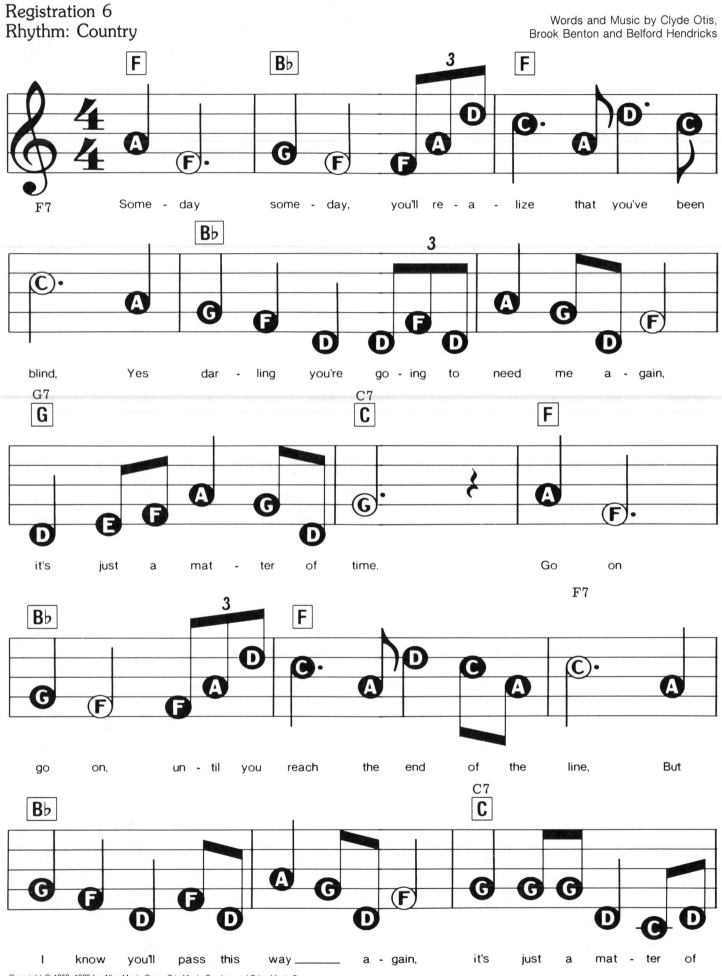

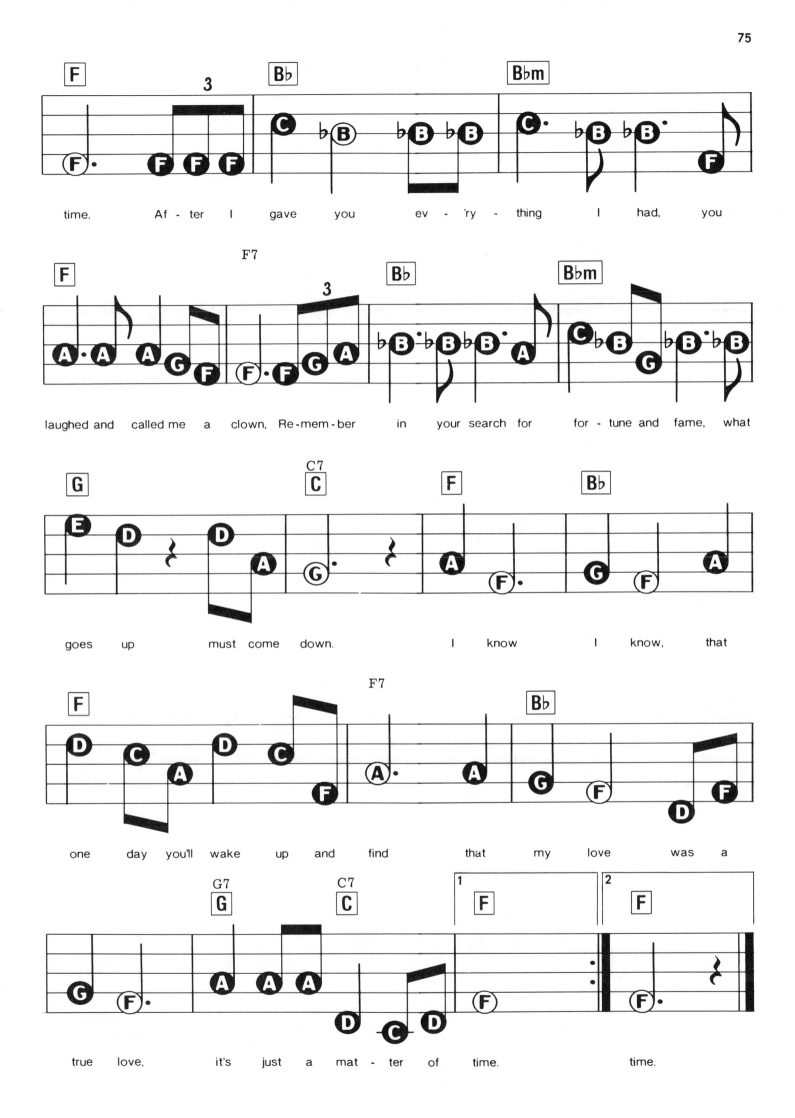

# Just In Time
### (From "BELLS ARE RINGING")

Registration 2
Rhythm: Fox Trot or Swing

Words by Betty Comden and Adolph Green
Music by Jule Styne

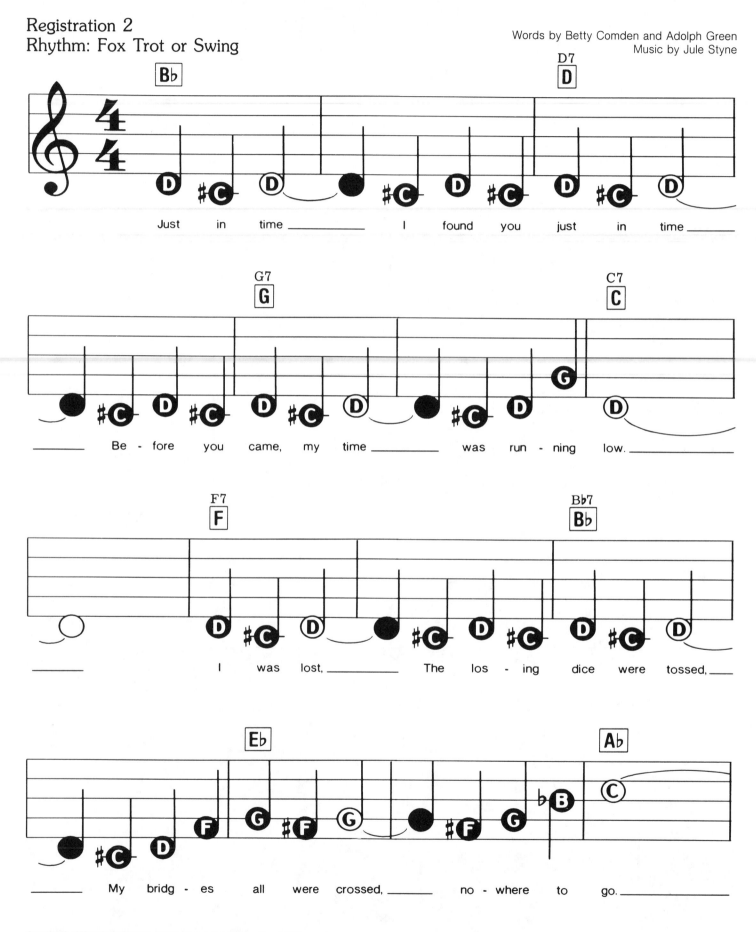

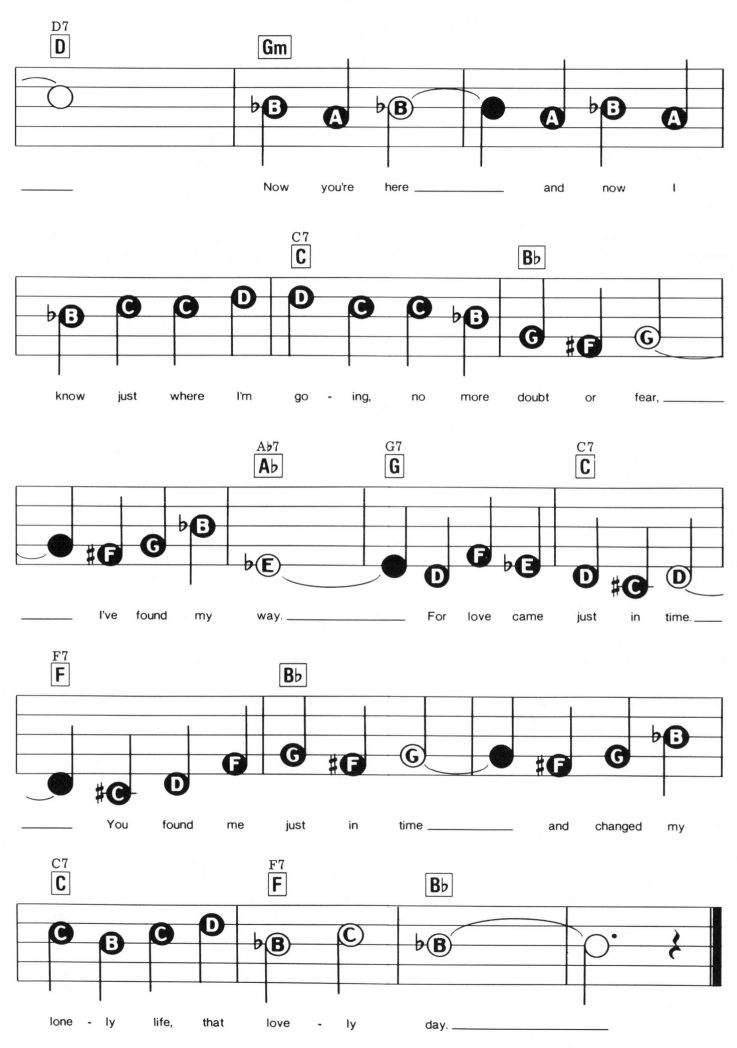

# Love Me Tender

Registration 9
Rhythm: Slow Rock or Rock

Words and Music by
Elvis Presley and Vera Matson

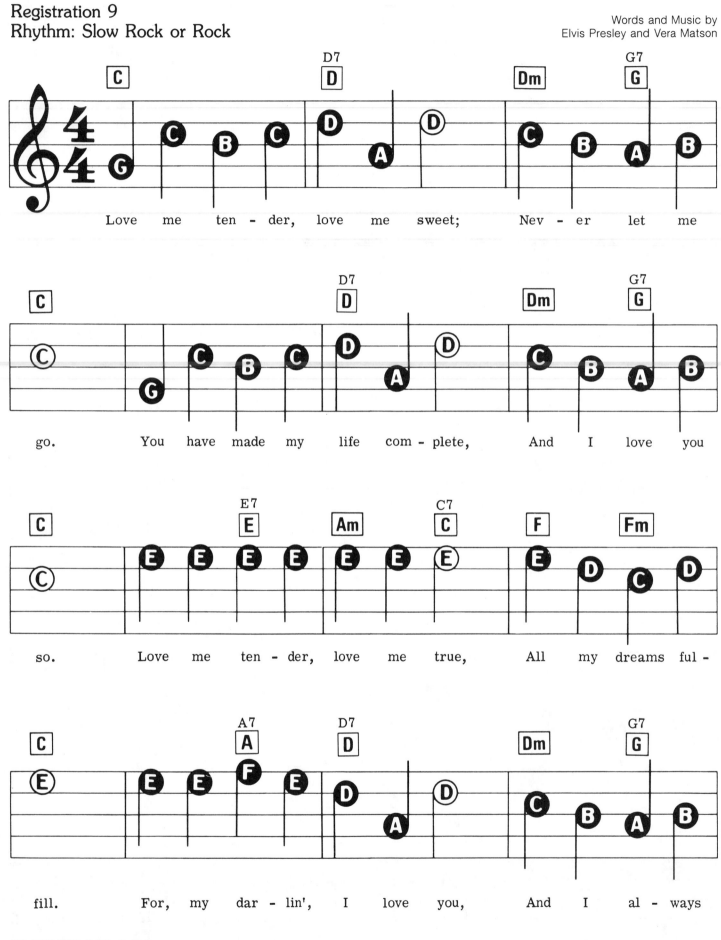

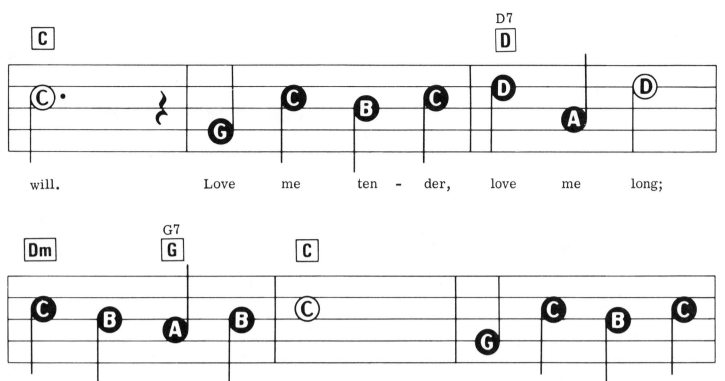

will. Love me ten - der, love me long;

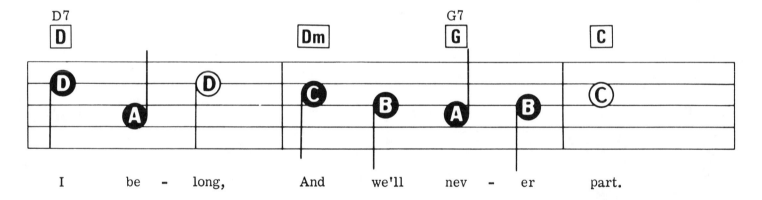

Take me to your heart. For it's there that

I be - long, And we'll nev - er part.

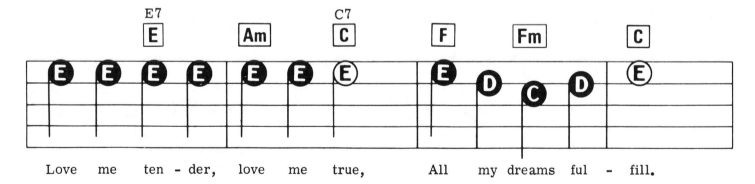

Love me ten - der, love me true, All my dreams ful - fill.

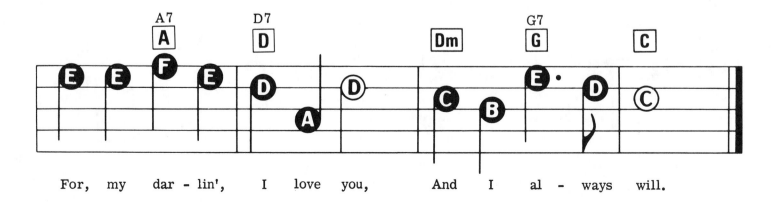

For, my dar - lin', I love you, And I al - ways will.

# Misty

Registration 8
Rhythm: Swing or Jazz

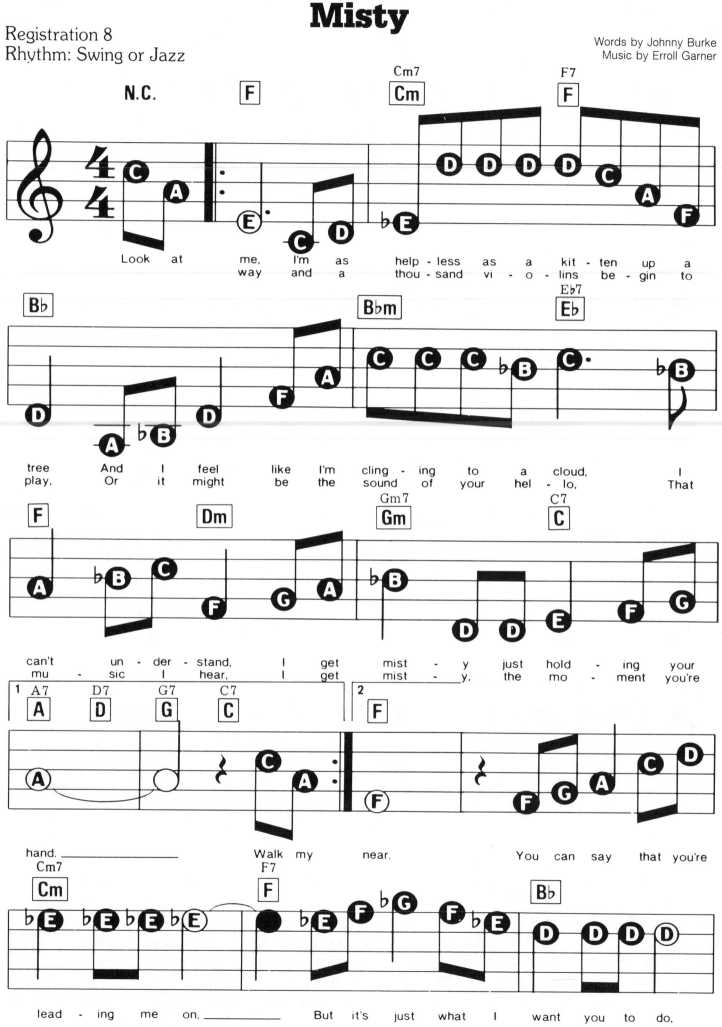

(Put Another Nickel In)

# Music! Music! Music!

Registration 4
Rhythm: Polka or March

Words and Music by
Stephan Weiss & Bernie Baum

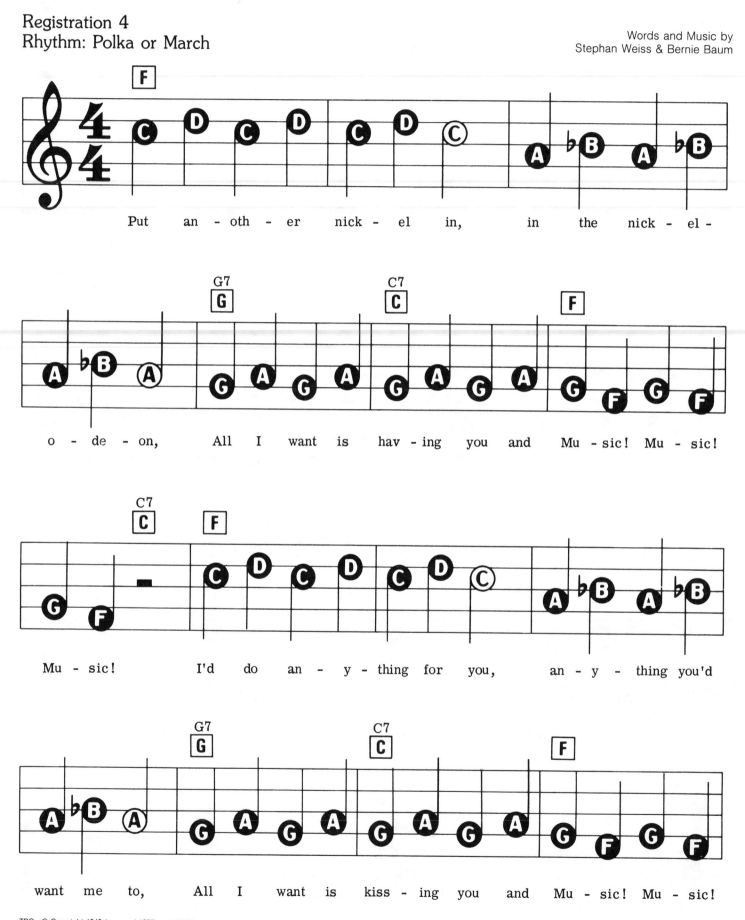

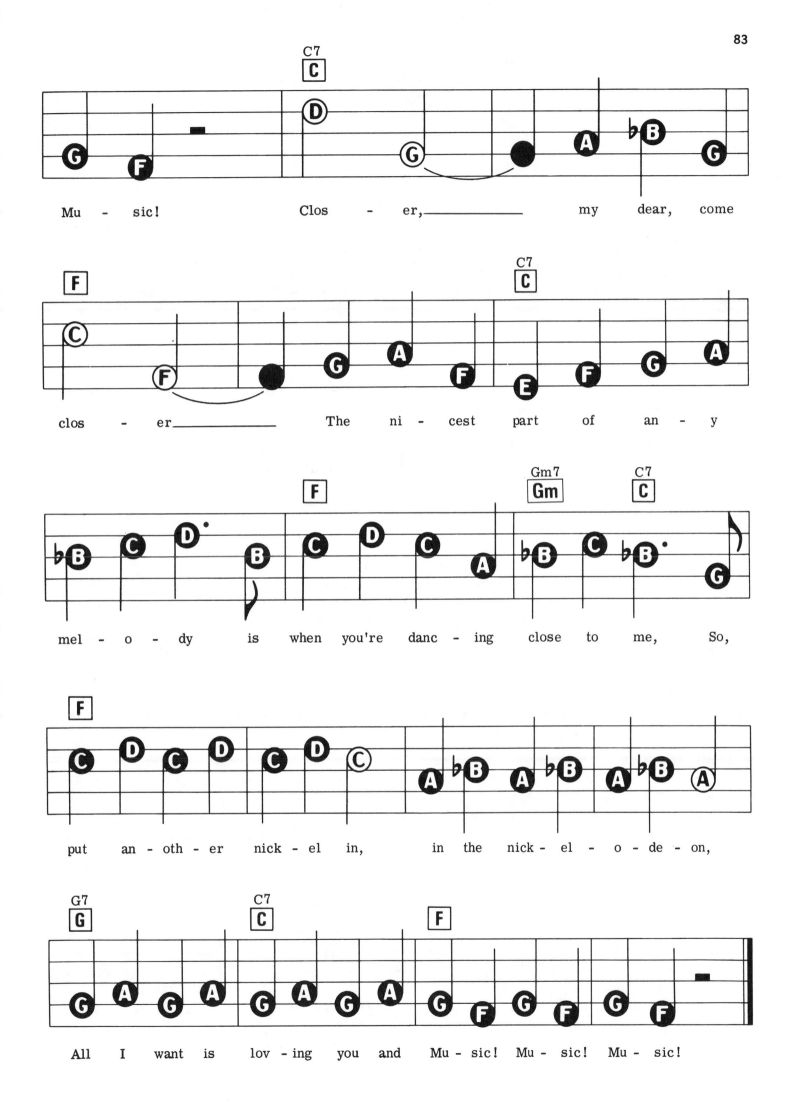

# Oh! My Pa-Pa
## (O Mein Papa)*

Registration 7
Rhythm: Swing

English Words by John Turner and Geoffrey Parsons
Music and Orginal Lyric by Paul Burkhard

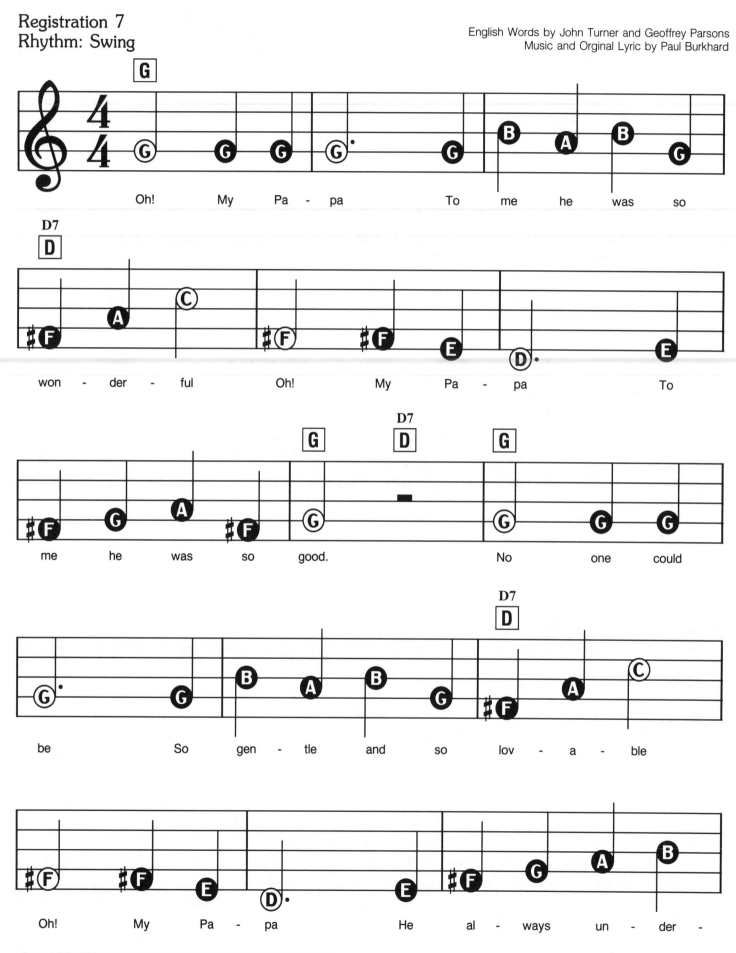

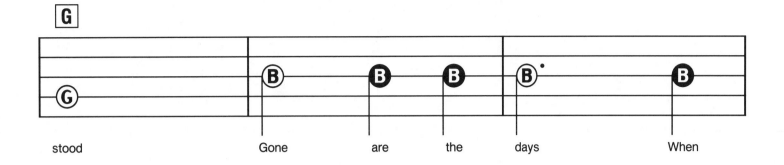

stood          Gone     are     the     days        When

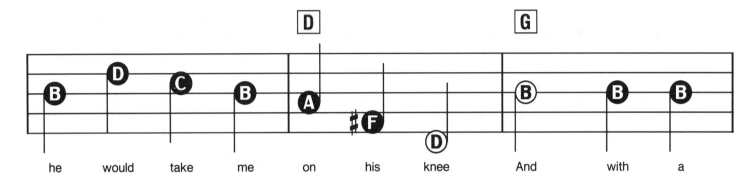

he     would   take   me     on     his     knee      And     with     a

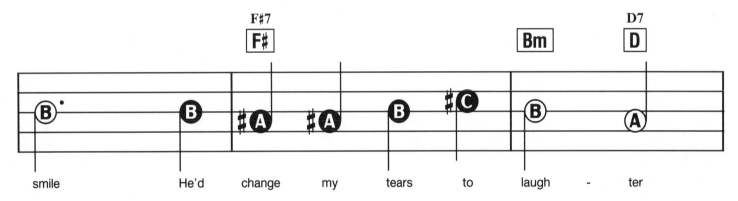

smile        He'd   change   my     tears   to     laugh  -  ter

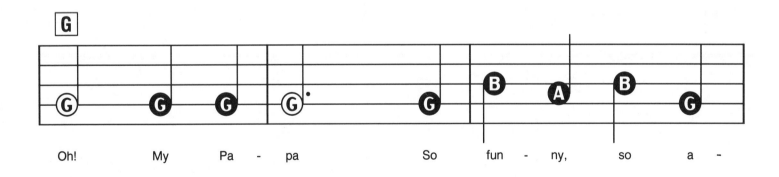

Oh!     My     Pa  -  pa          So     fun  -  ny,   so   a -

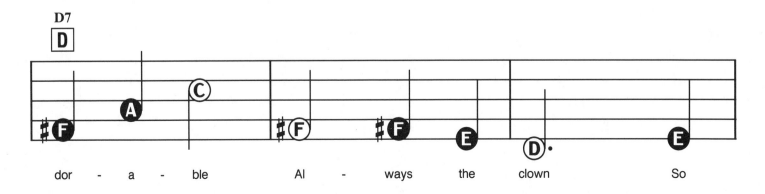

dor  -  a  -  ble     Al  -  ways   the   clown     So

85

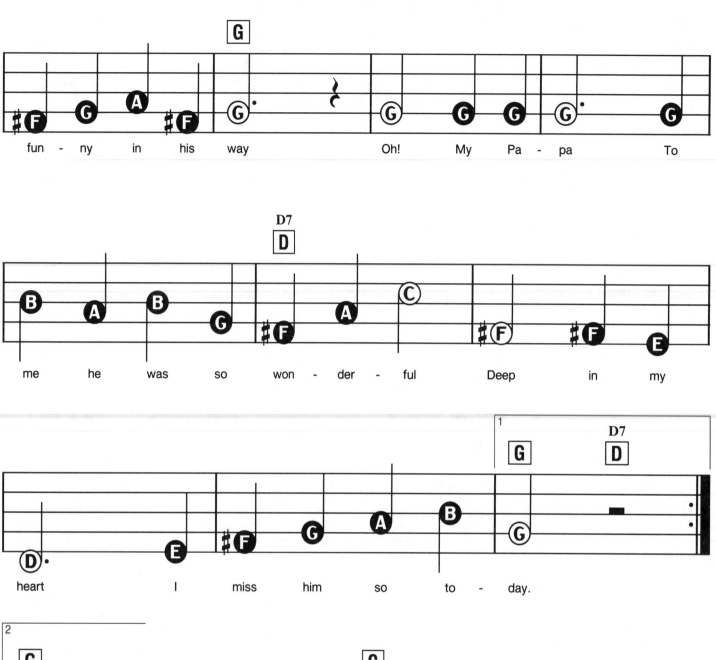

fun - ny in his way Oh! My Pa - pa To

me he was so won - der - ful Deep in my

heart I miss him so to - day.

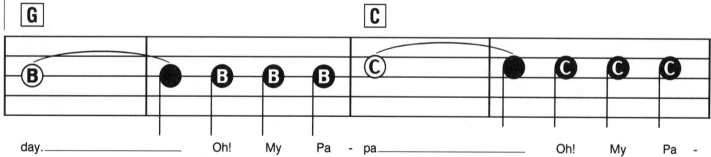

day._____ Oh! My Pa - pa_____ Oh! My Pa -

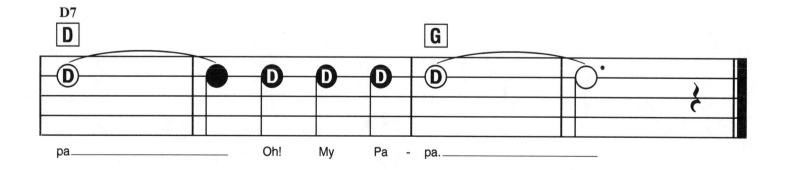

pa_____ Oh! My Pa - pa._____

# That's All

Registration 10
Rhythm: Ballad

Words and Music by
Alan Brandt and Bob Haymes

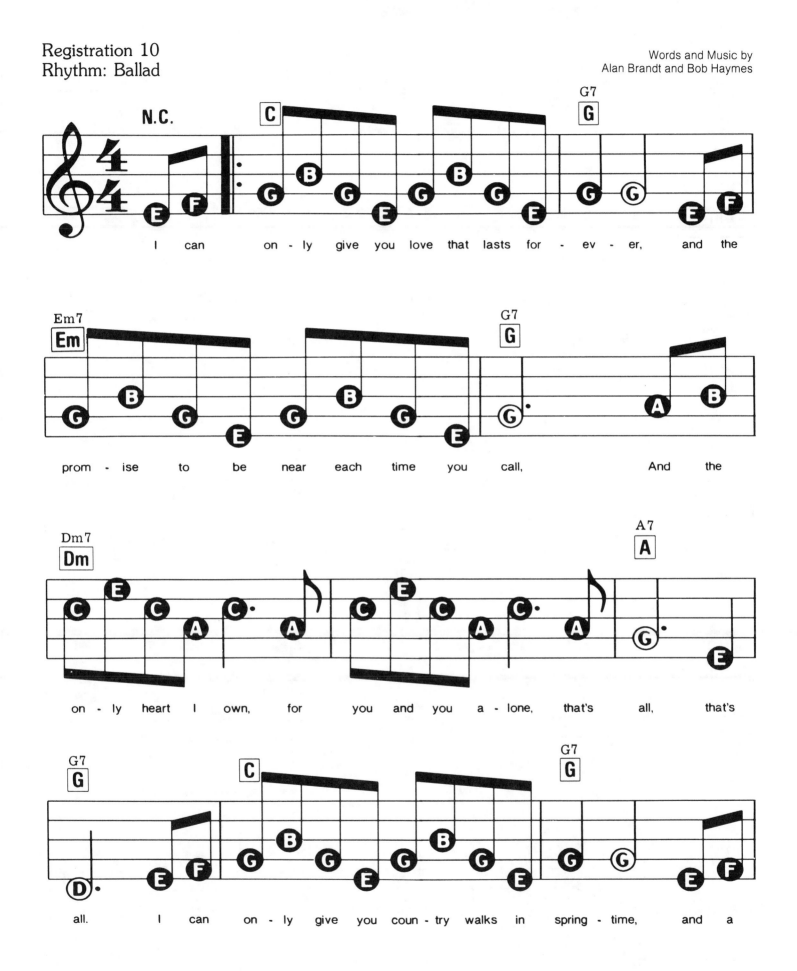

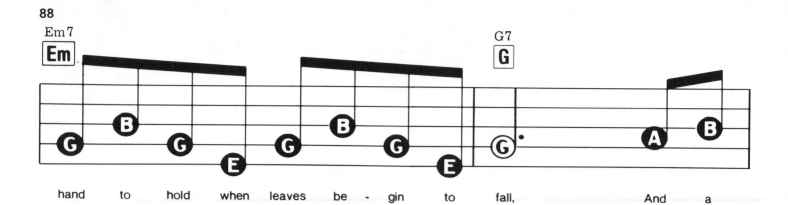

hand    to    hold    when    leaves    be - gin    to    fall,    And    a

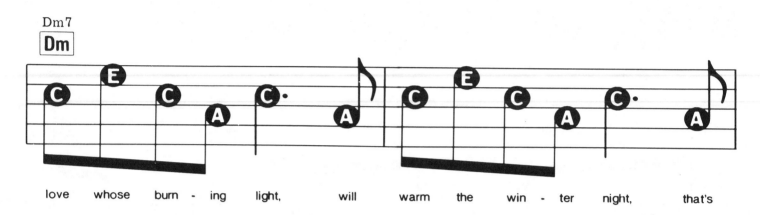

love    whose    burn - ing    light,    will    warm    the    win - ter    night,    that's

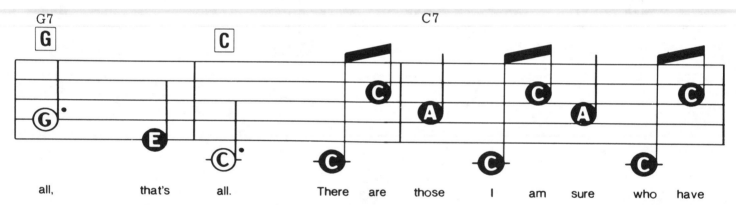

all,    that's    all.    There    are    those    I    am    sure    who    have

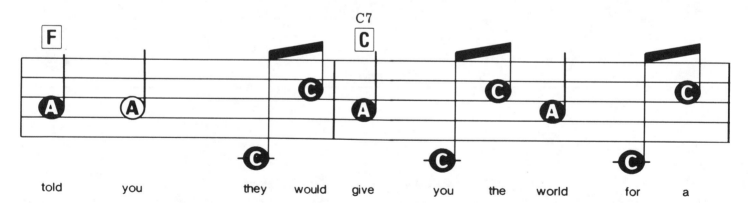

told    you    they    would    give    you    the    world    for    a

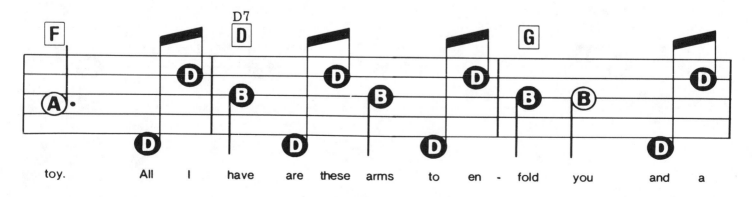

toy.    All    I    have    are    these    arms    to    en - fold    you    and    a

89

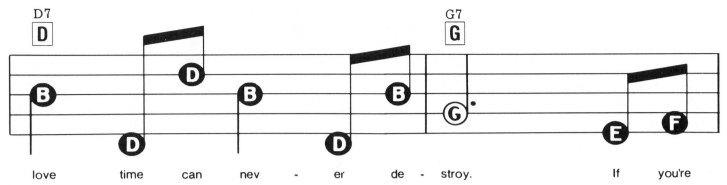

love time can nev - er de - stroy. If you're

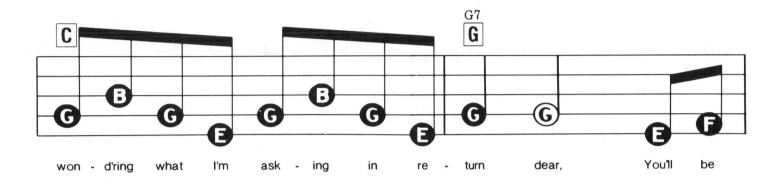

won - d'ring what I'm ask - ing in re - turn dear, You'll be

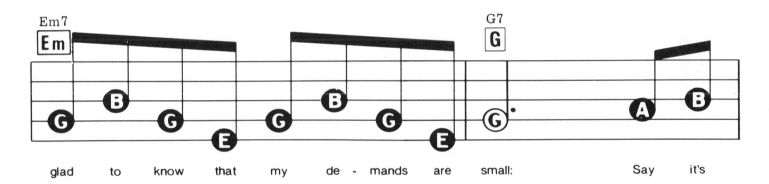

glad to know that my de - mands are small: Say it's

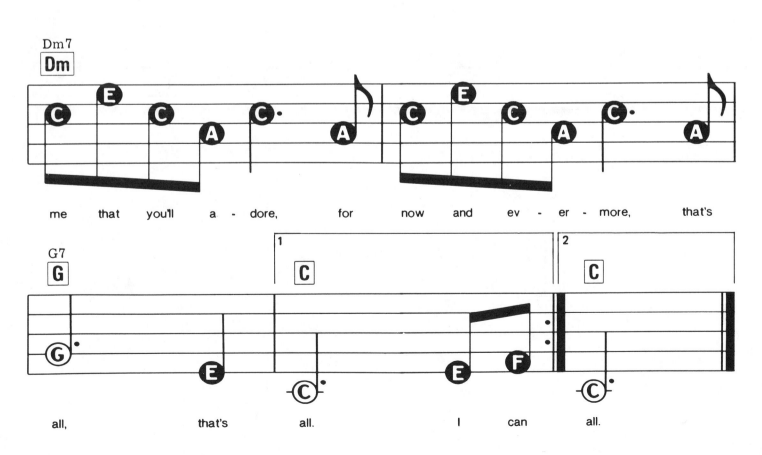

me that you'll a - dore, for now and ev - er - more, that's

all, that's all. I can all.

# Old Cape Cod

Registration 8
Rhythm: Ballad

Words and Music by Claire Rothrock,
Milt Yakus and Allan Jeffrey

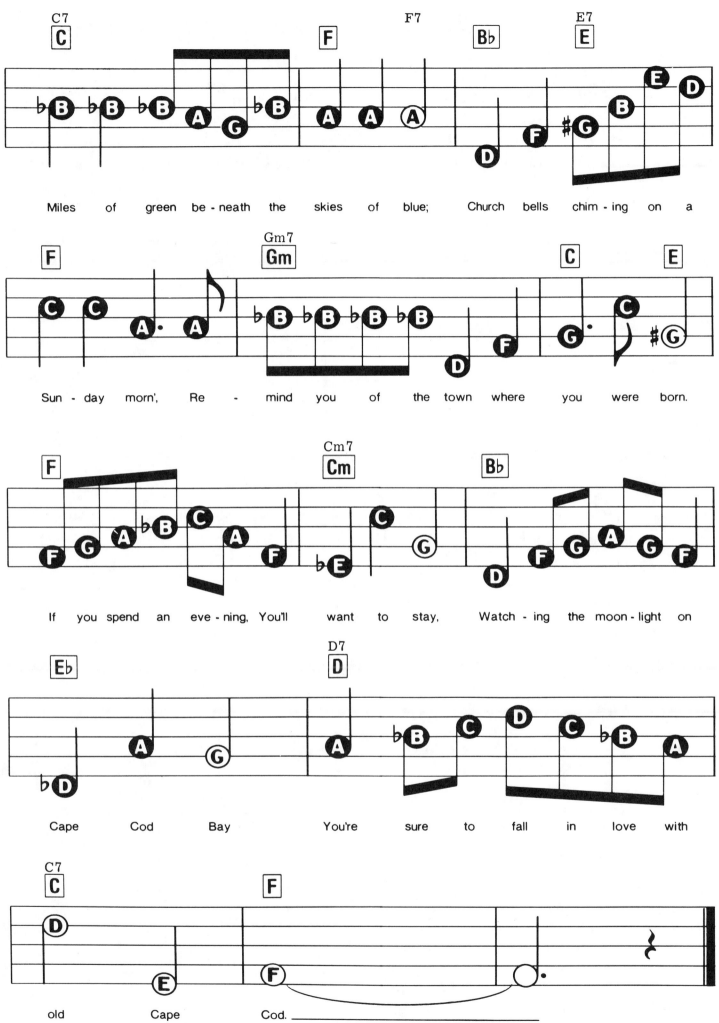

# On The Street Where You Live

(From "MY FAIR LADY")

Registration 4
Rhythm: Beguine

Words by Alan Jay Lerner
Music by Frederick Loewe

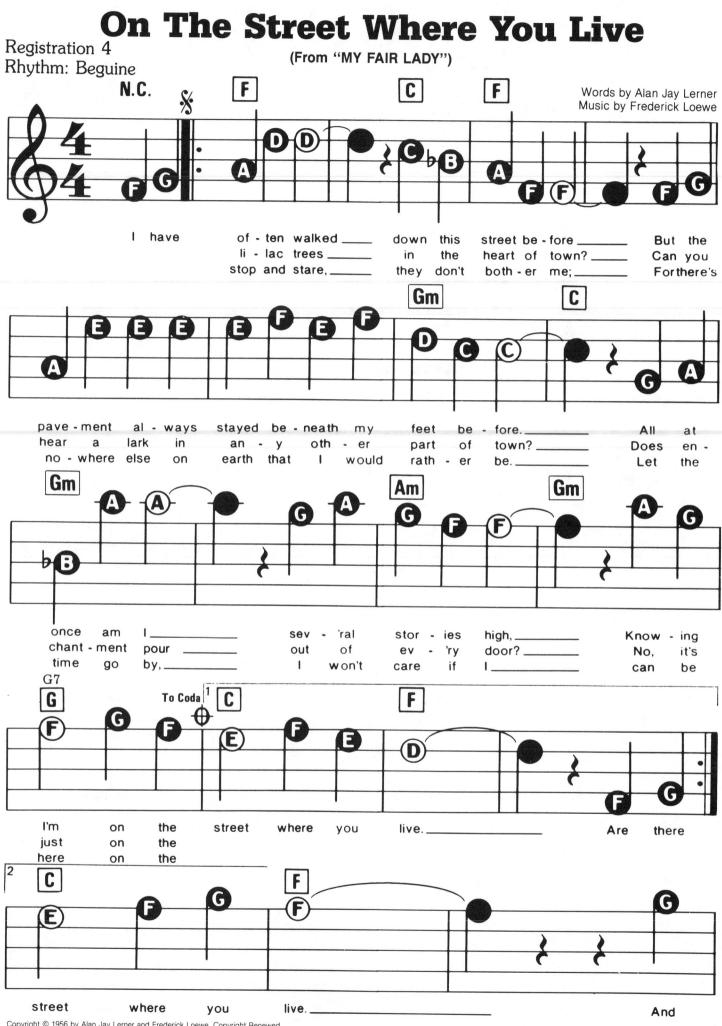

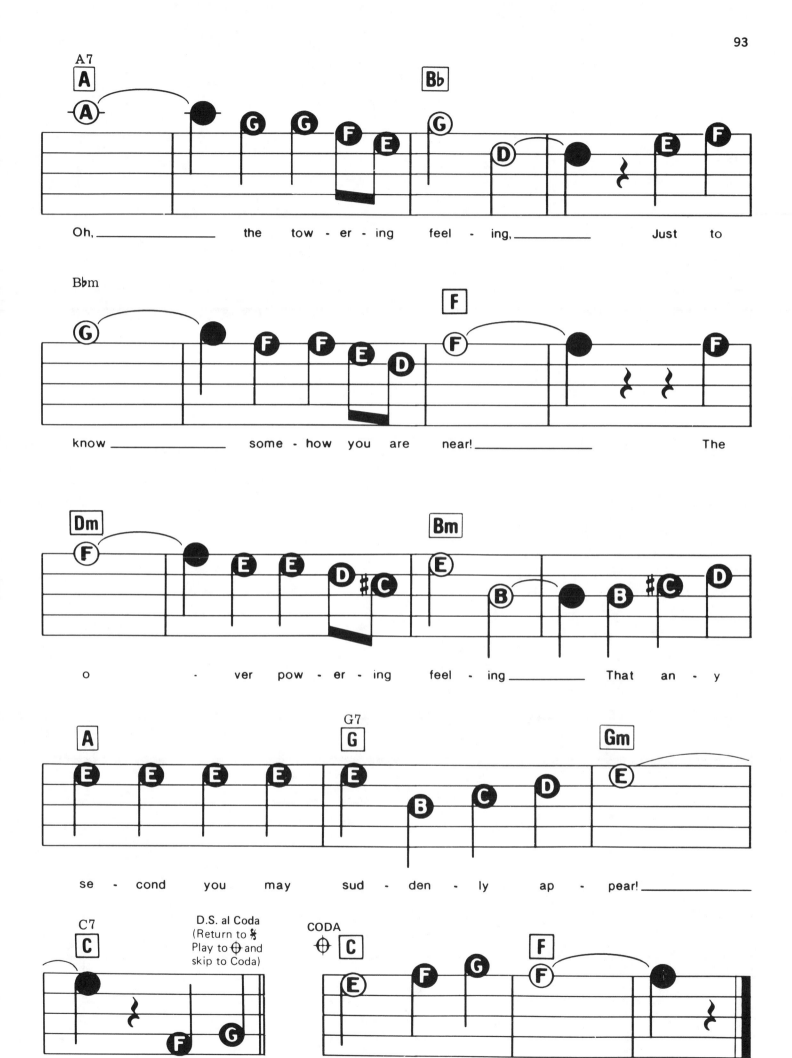

# Only You
## (And You Alone)

Registration 2
Rhythm: Swing

Words and Music by
Buck Ram and Ande Rand

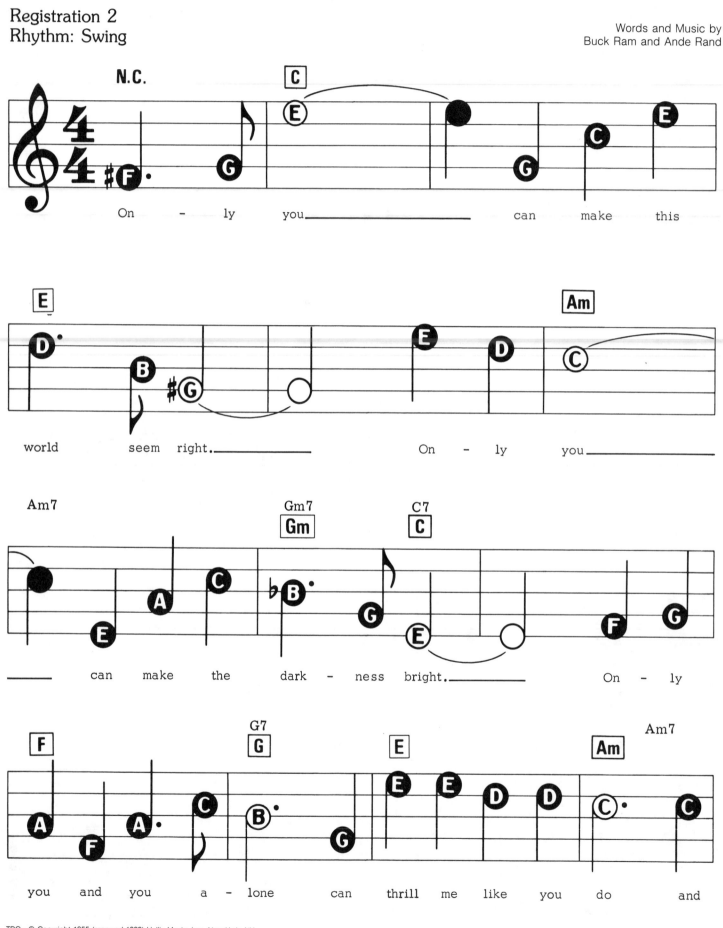

95

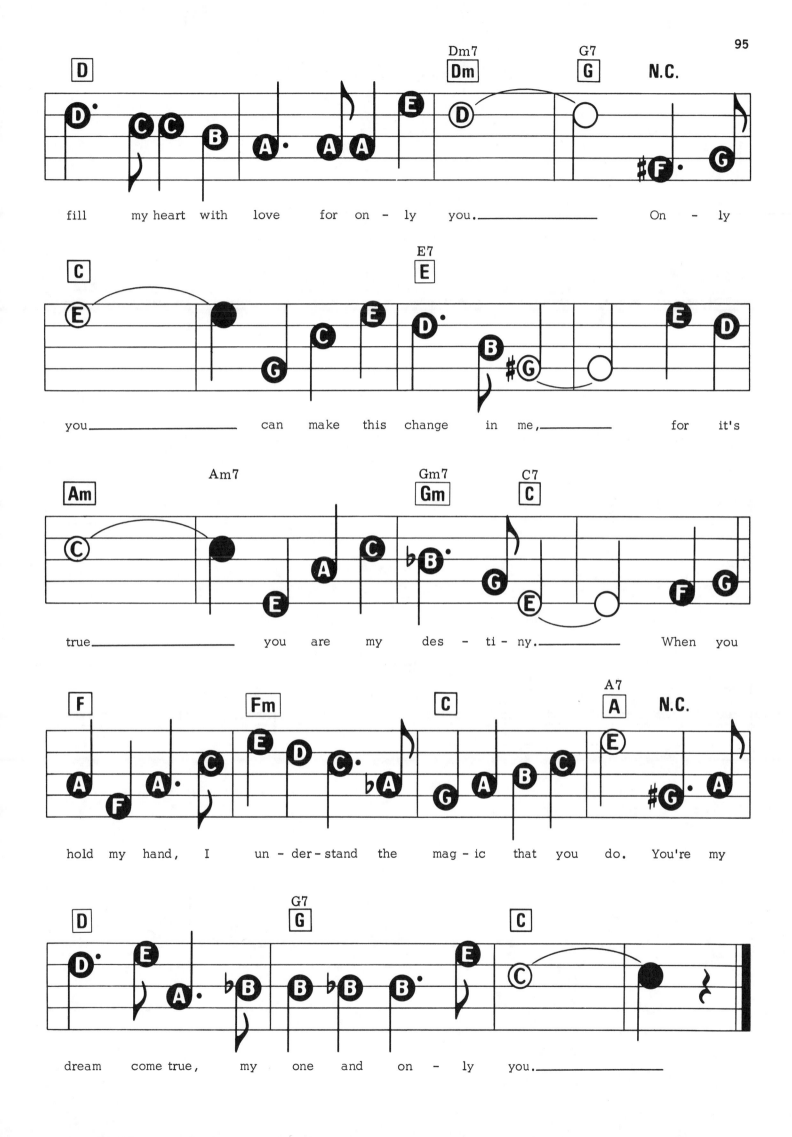

# The Party's Over

Registration 9
Rhythm: Fox Trot or Ballad

Words by Betty Comden and Adolph Green
Music by Jule Styne

# Que Sera, Sera
## (Whatever Will Be, Will Be)

Registration 10
Rhythm: Waltz

Words and Music by
Jay Livingston and Ray Evans

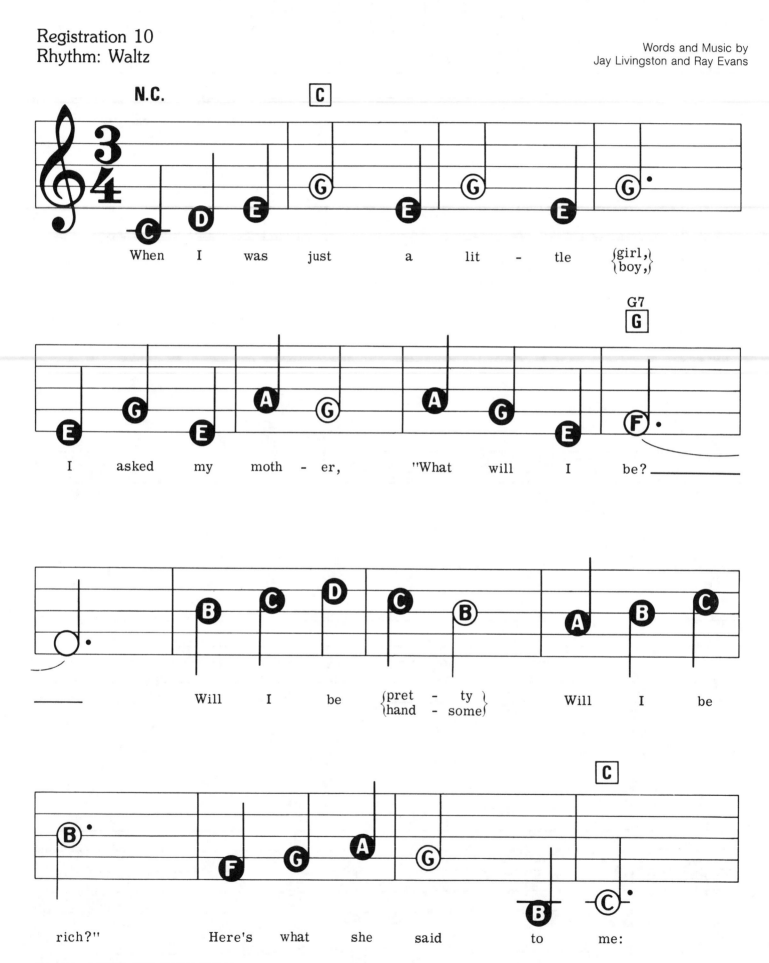

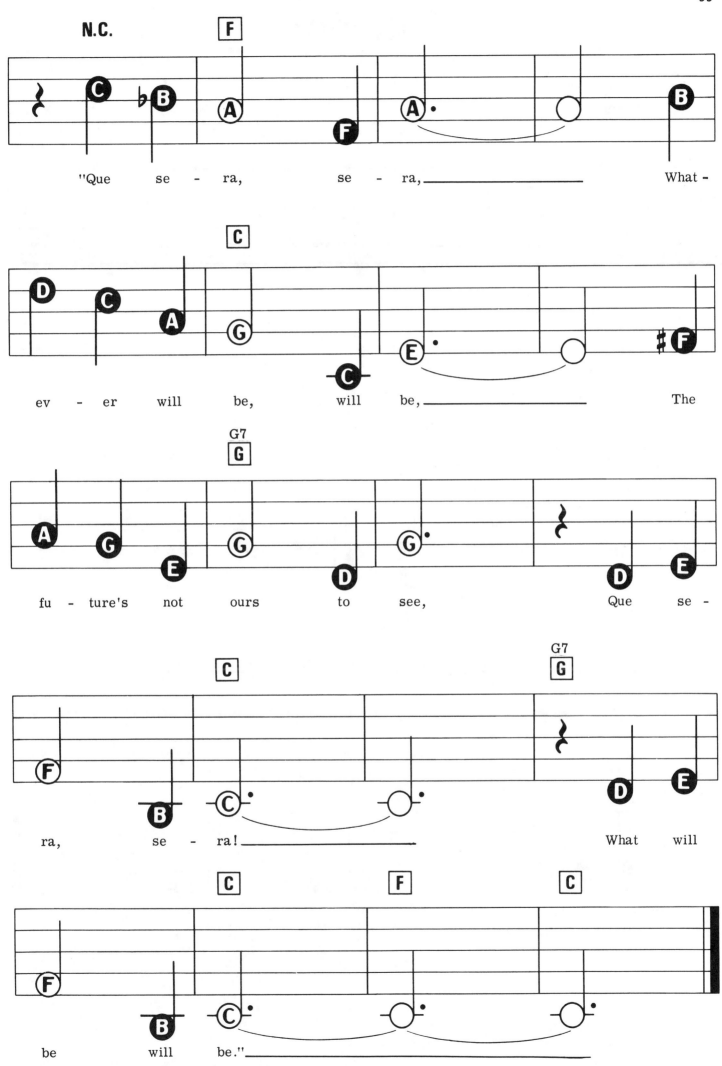

# Rag Mop

Registration 5
Rhythm: Swing

Words and Music by
Johnnie Lee Wills and Deacon Anderson

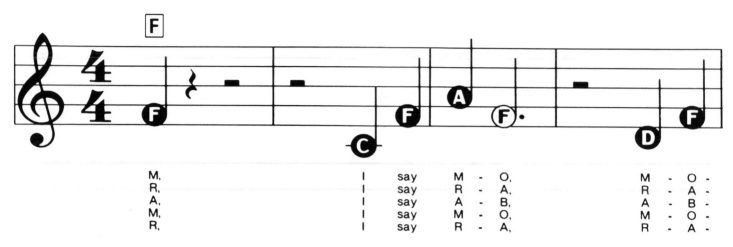

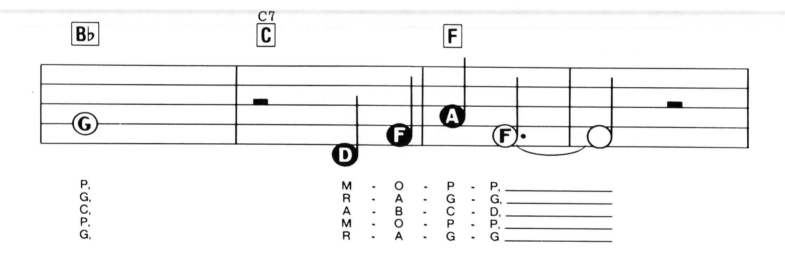

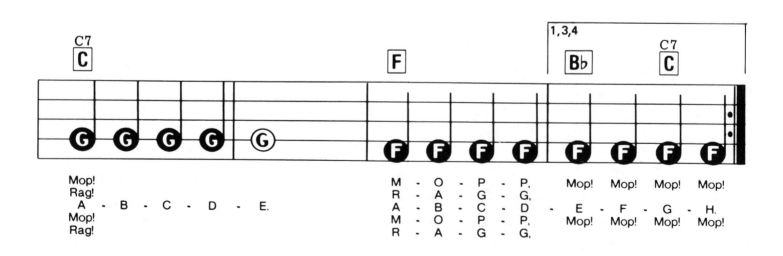

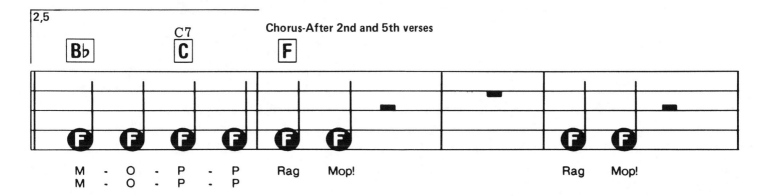

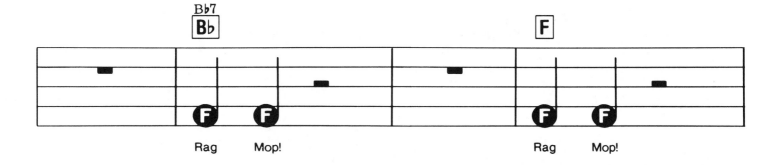

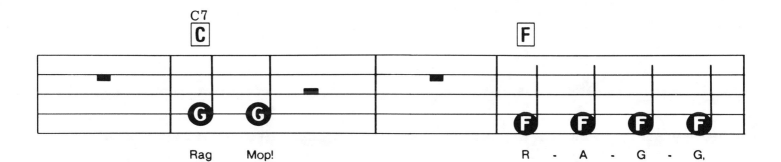

# Rock Around The Clock

Registration 8
Rhythm: Rock

By Max C. Freedman and Jimmy DeKnight

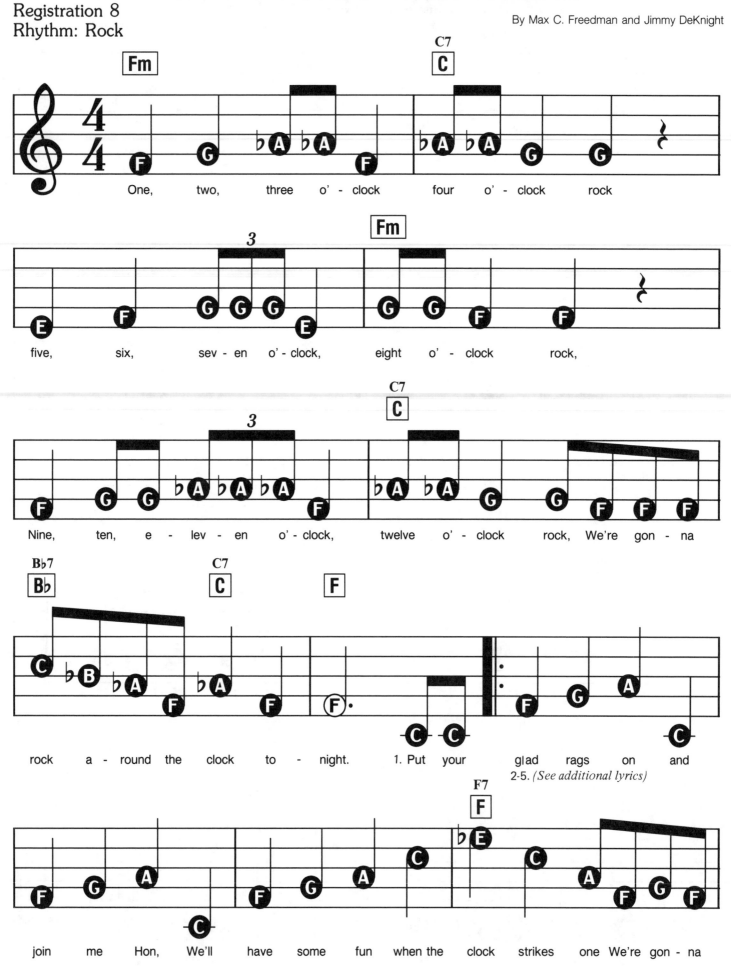

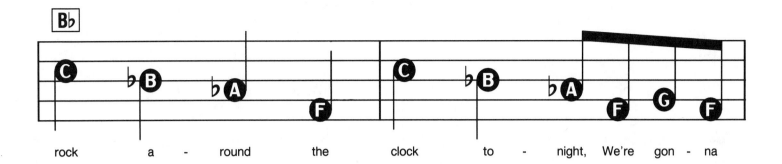

rock a - round the clock to - night, We're gon - na

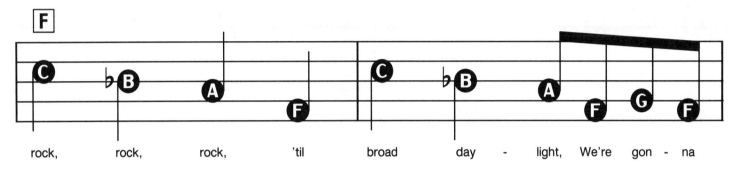

rock, rock, rock, 'til broad day - light, We're gon - na

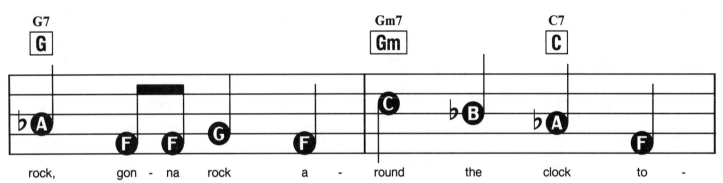

rock, gon - na rock a - round the clock to -

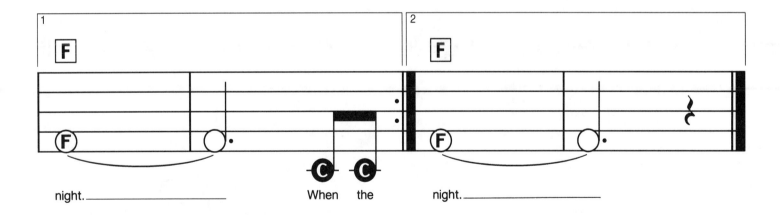

night._____ When the night._____

## Additional Lyrics

2. When the clock strikes two, and three and four,
   If the band slows down we'll yell for more,
   We're gonna rock around the clock tonight,
   We're gonna rock, rock, rock, etc....

3. When the chimes ring five and six and seven,
   We'll be rockin' up in seventh heav'n,
   We're gonna rock around the clock tonight,
   We're gonna rock, rock, rock, etc....

4. When it's eight, nine, ten, eleven, too,
   I'll be goin' strong and so will you,
   We're gonna rock around the clock tonight,
   We're gonna rock, rock, rock, etc....

5. When the clock strikes twelve, we'll cool off, then,
   Start a rockin' 'round the clock again,
   We're gonna rock around the clock tonight,
   We're gonna rock, rock, rock, etc....

# Satin Doll

Registration 4
Rhythm: Swing or Jazz

By Duke Ellington, Johnny Mercer
and Billy Strayhorn

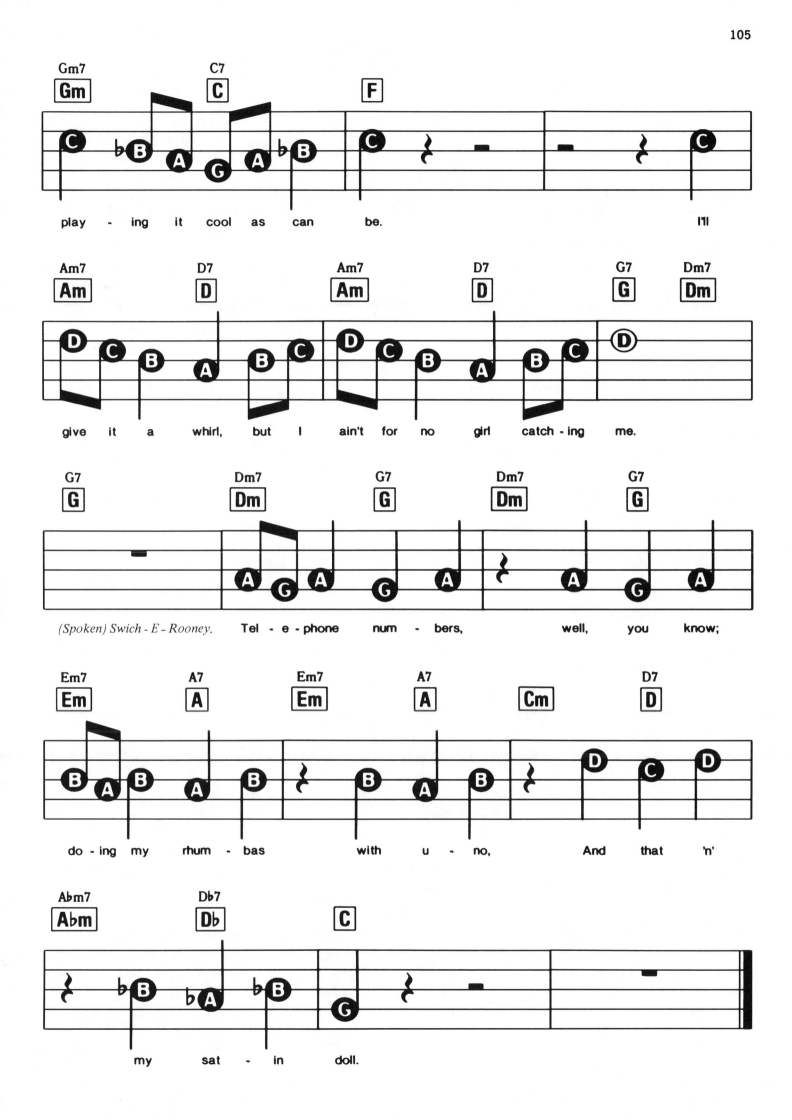

# Sh-Boom
## (Life Could Be A Dream)

Registration 1
Rhythm: Slow Rock or Ballad

Words and Music by James Keyes,
Claude Feaster, Carl Feaster,
Floyd McRae and James Edwards

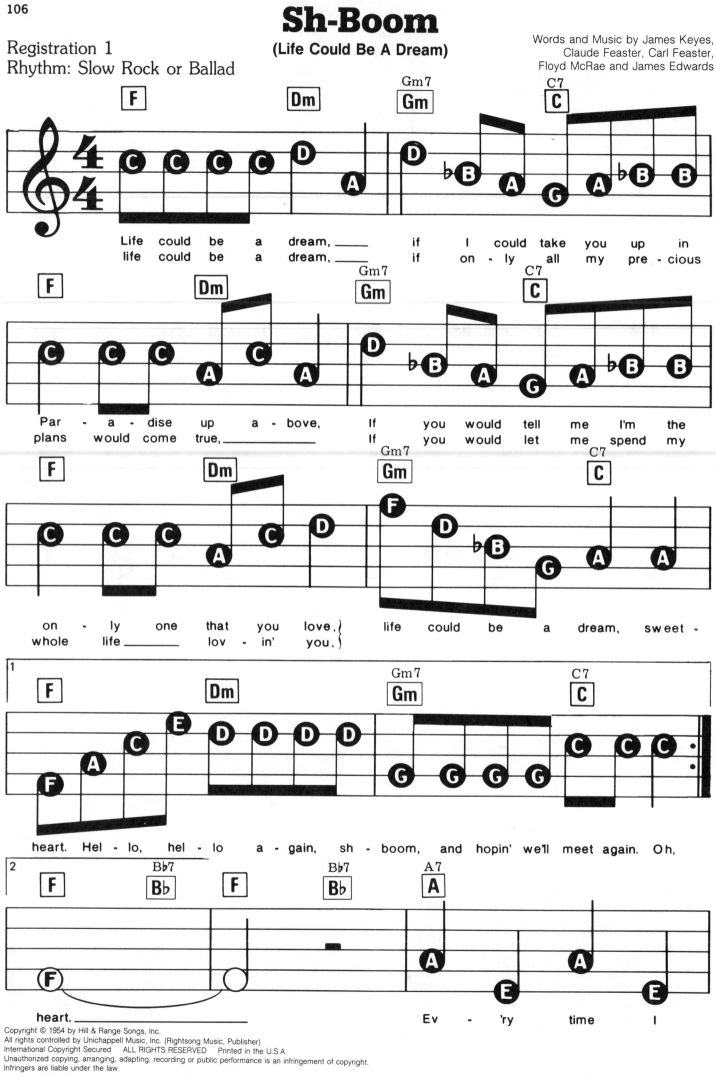

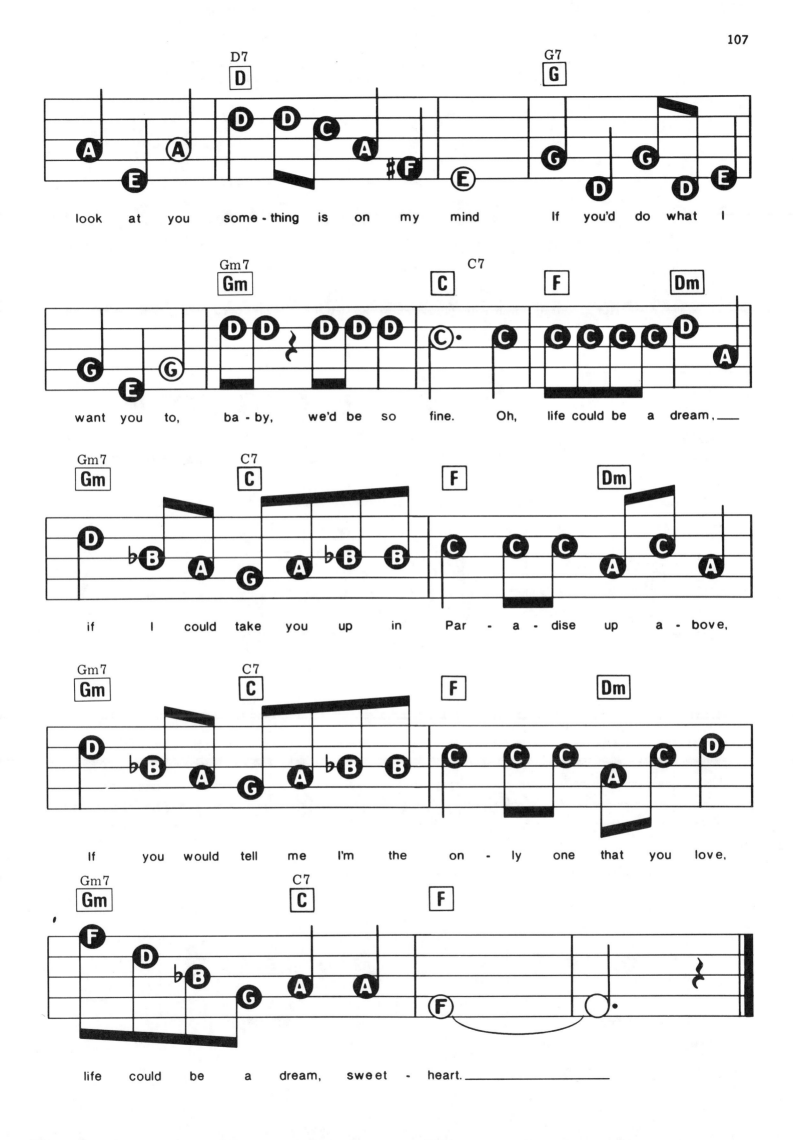

# Shake, Rattle And Roll

Registration 8
Rhythm: Rock or Jazz Rock

Words and Music by
Charles Calhoun

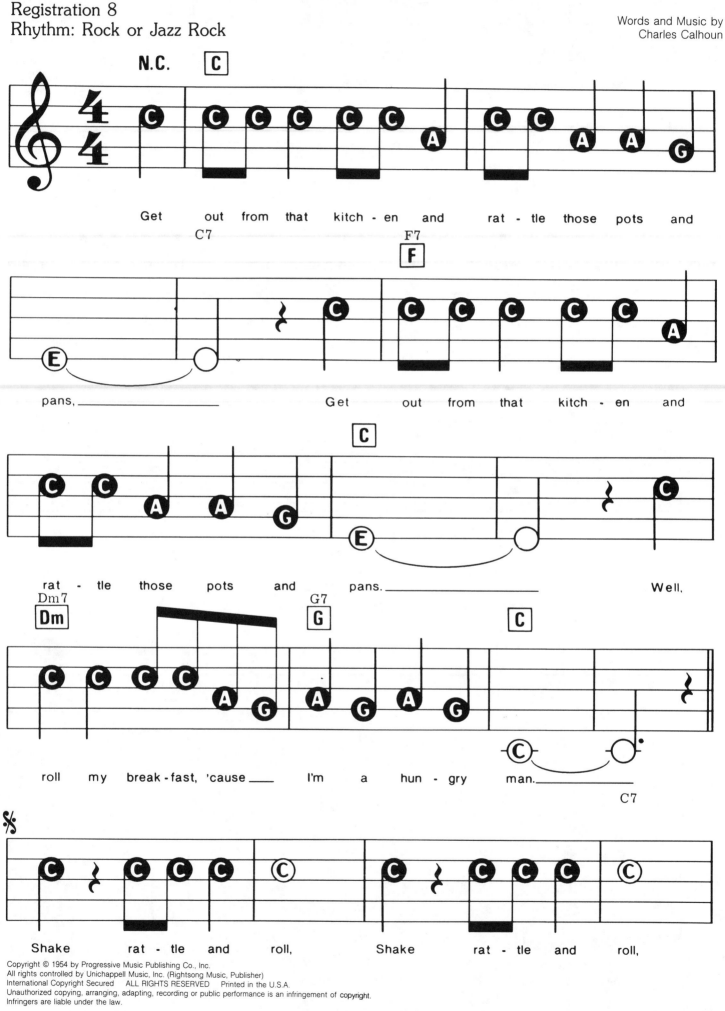

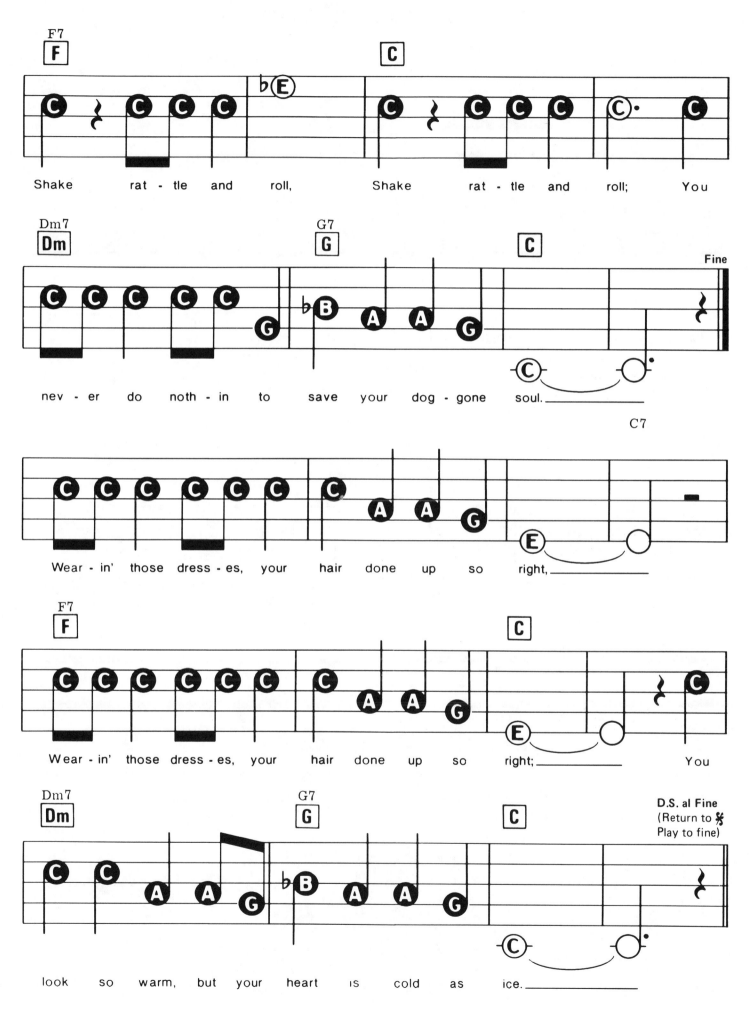

# Sixteen Tons

Registration 9
Rhythm: Rock

Words and Music by
Merle Travis

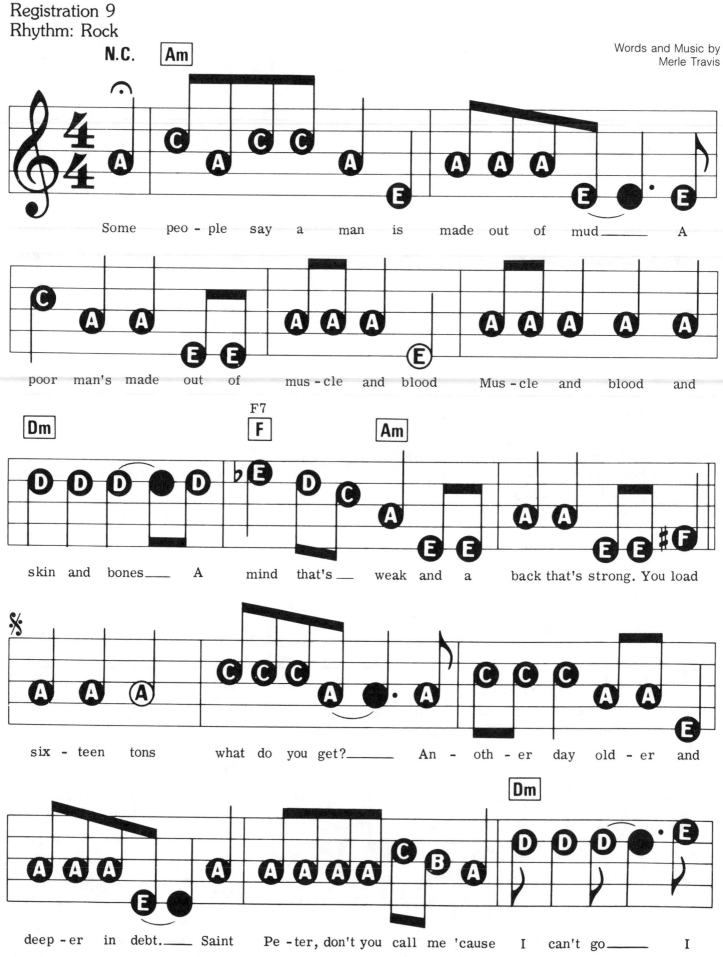

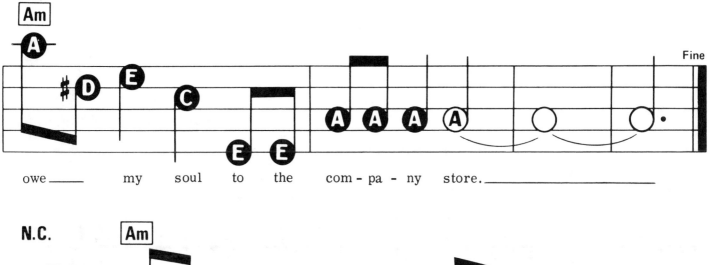

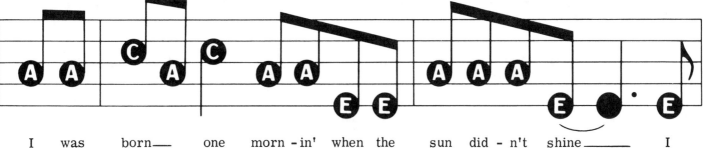

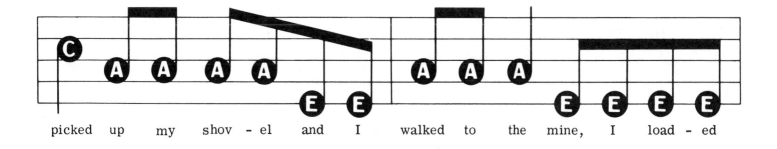

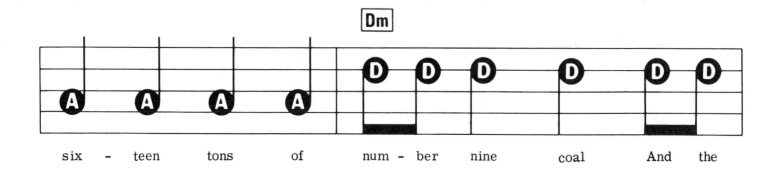

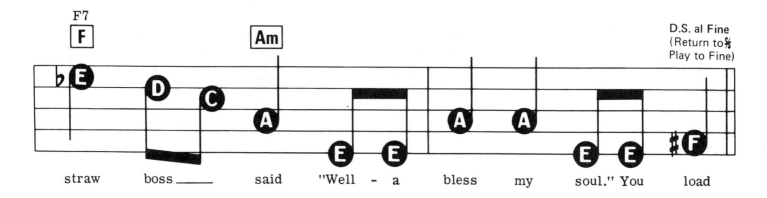

# Smile
### (Theme From "MODERN TIMES")

Registration 9
Rhythm: Fox Trot or Ballad

Words by John Turner and Geoffrey Parsons
Music by Charles Chaplin

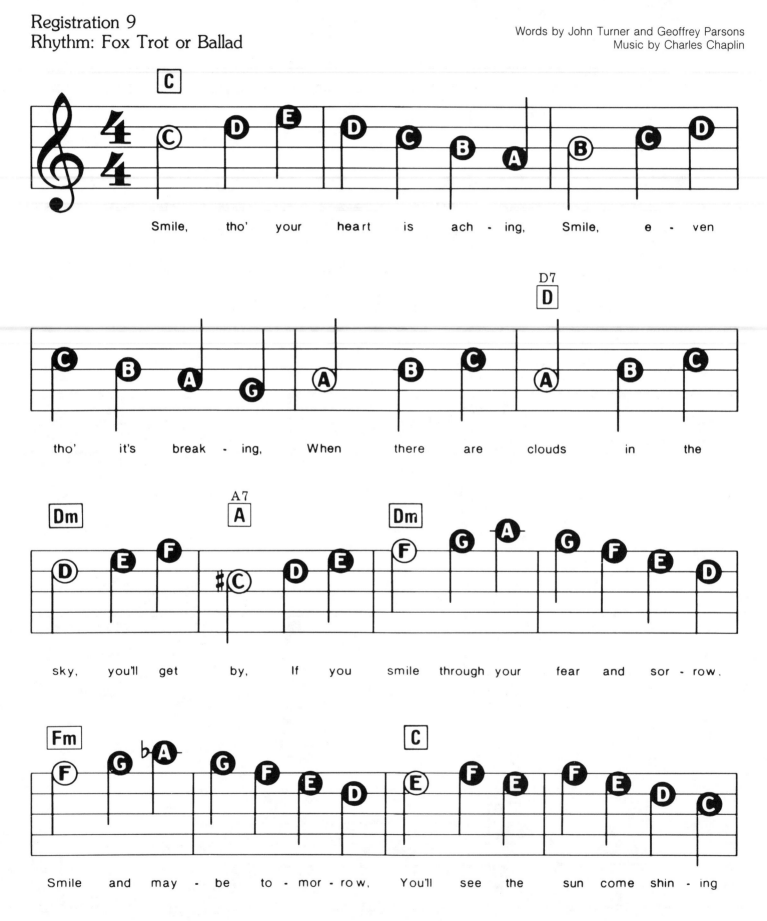

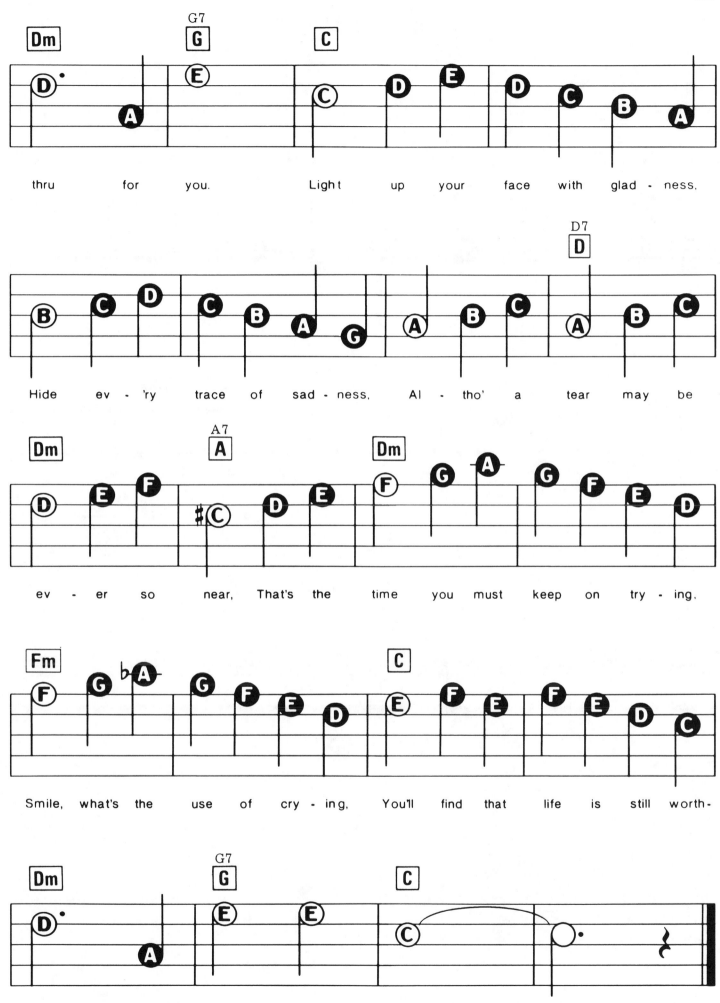

# Tammy

Registration 3
Rhythm: Waltz

Words and Music by
Jay Livingston and Ray Evans

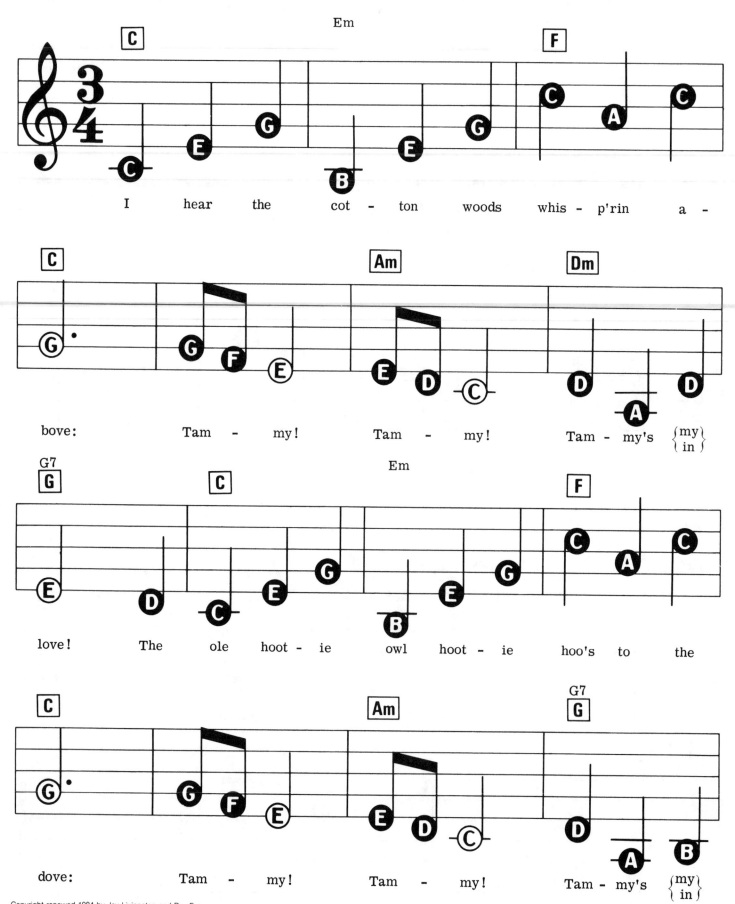

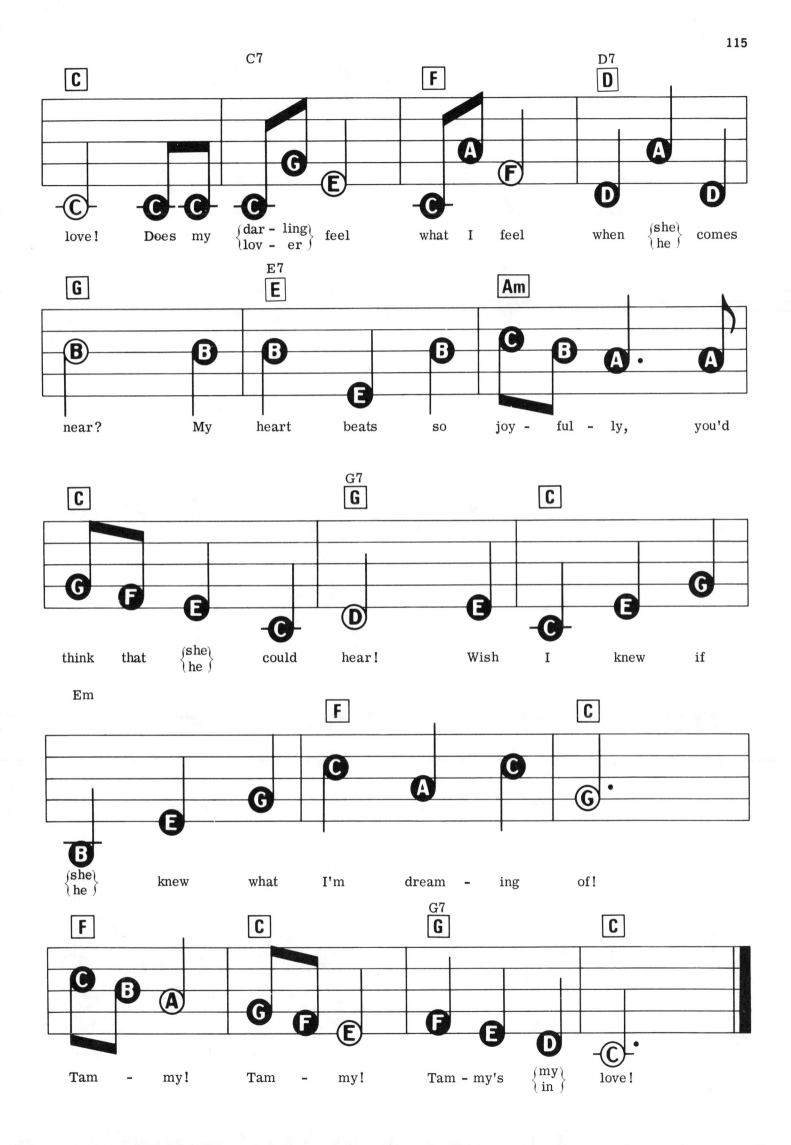

# They Call The Wind Maria

### (From "PAINT YOUR WAGON")

Registration 1
Rhythm: Country

Words by Alan Jay Lerner
Music by Frederick Loewe

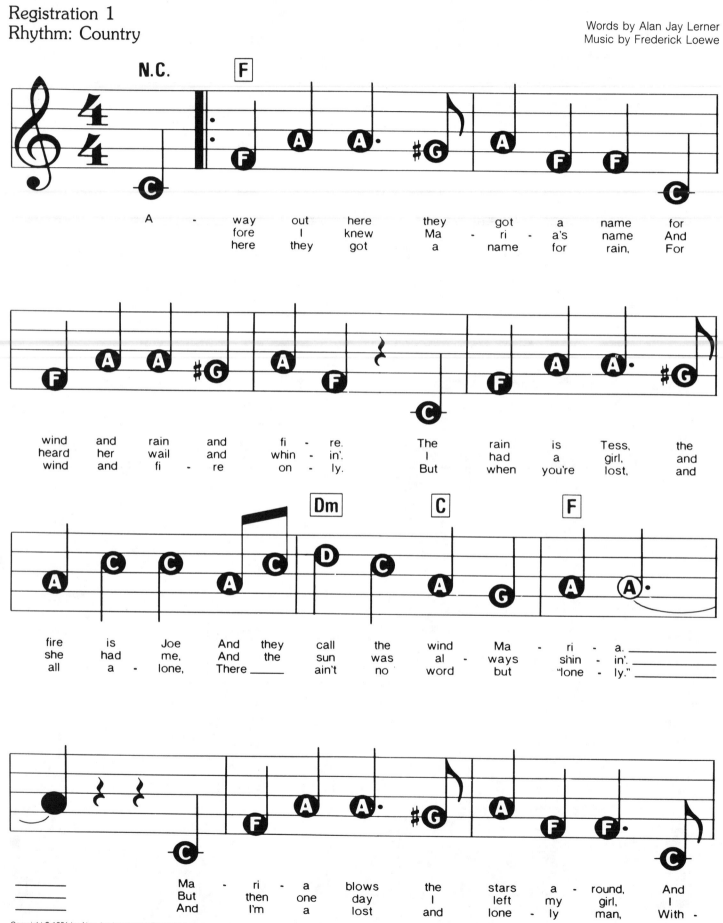

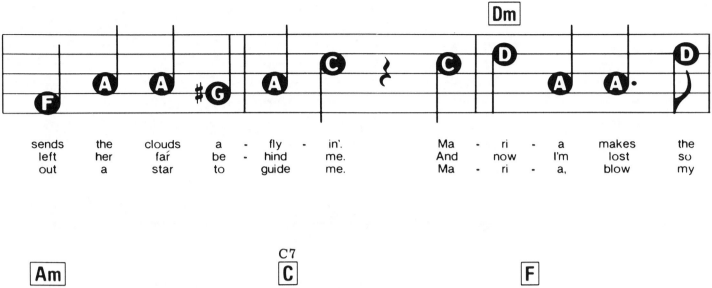

sends the clouds a - fly - in'.
left her far be - hind me.
out a star to guide me.

Ma - ri - a makes the
And now I'm lost so
Ma - ri - a, blow my

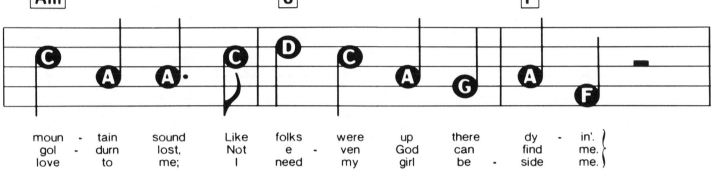

moun - tain sound
gol - durn lost,
love to me;

Like folks were up there dy - in'.
Not e - ven God can find me.
I need my girl be - side me.

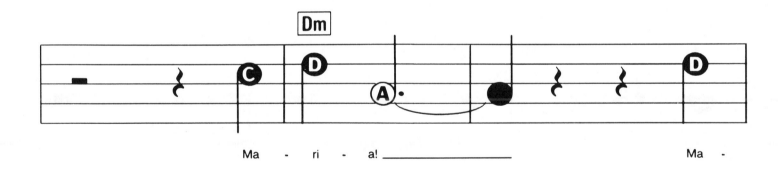

Ma - ri - a! _____ Ma -

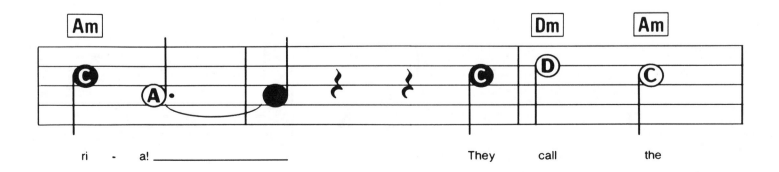

ri - a! _____ They call the

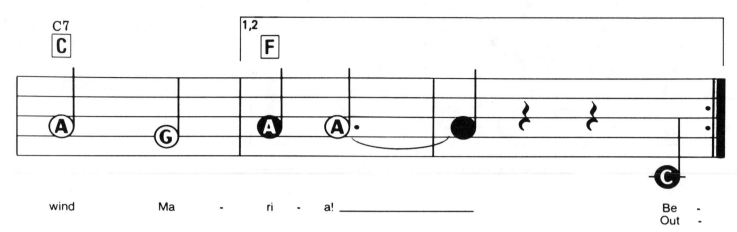

wind     Ma - ri - a! _____     Be -
Out -

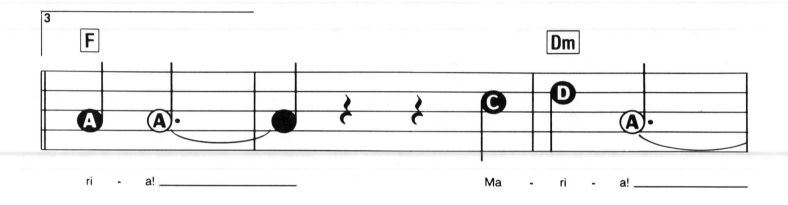

ri - a! _____     Ma - ri - a! _____

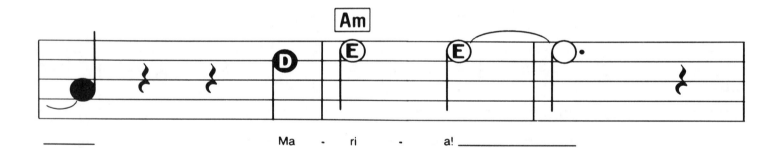

\_\_\_\_\_     Ma - ri - a! _____

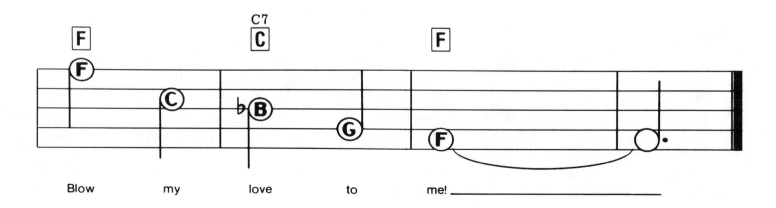

Blow     my     love     to     me! _____

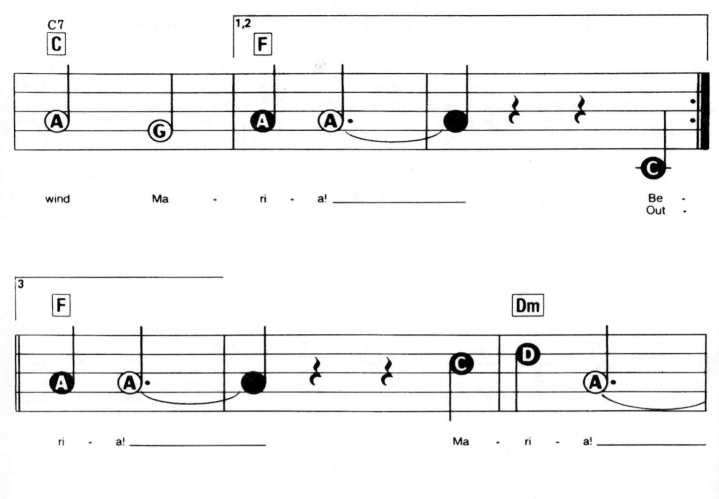

wind    Ma - ri - a! _____    Be -
Out -

ri - a! _____    Ma - ri - a! _____

_____    Ma - ri - a! _____

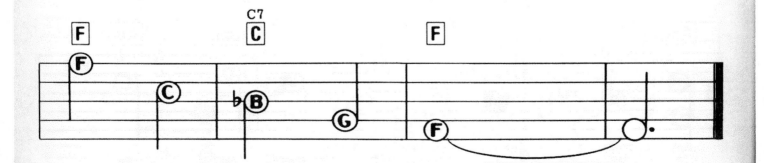

# Wheel Of Fortune

Registration 9
Rhythm: Swing

Words and Music by
Bennie Benjamin and George Weiss

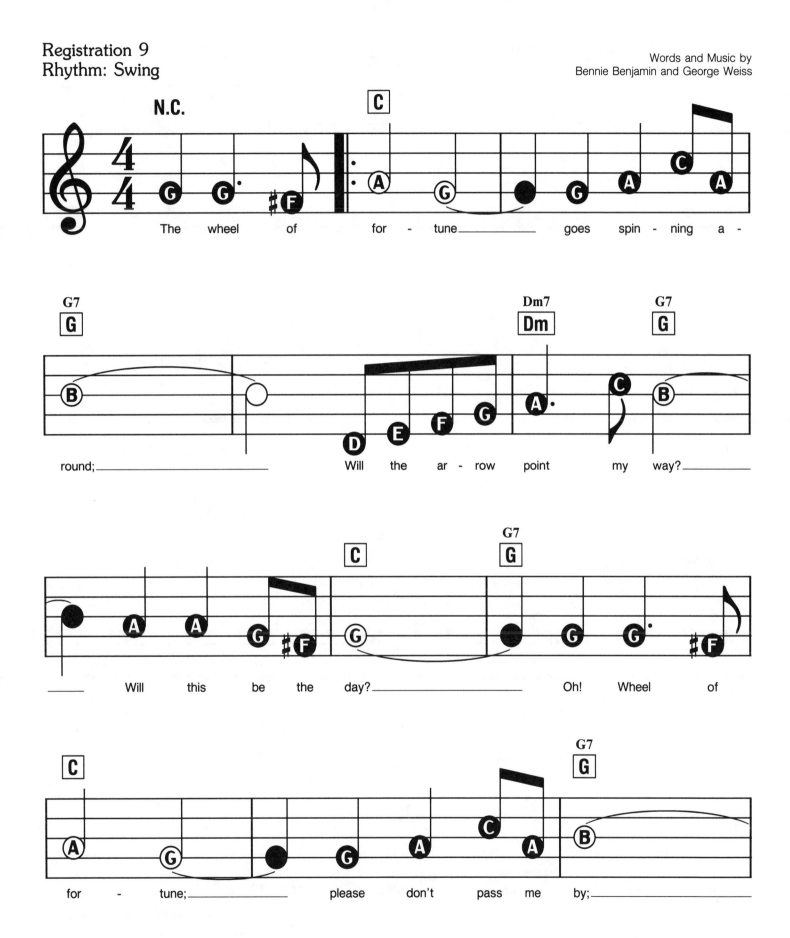

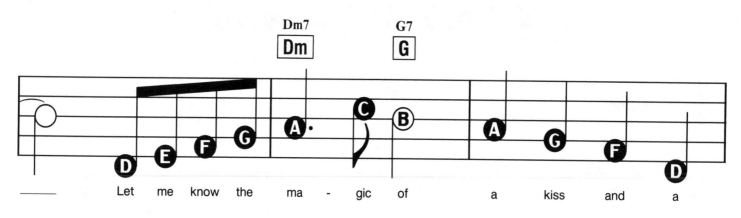

Let me know the ma - gic of a kiss and a

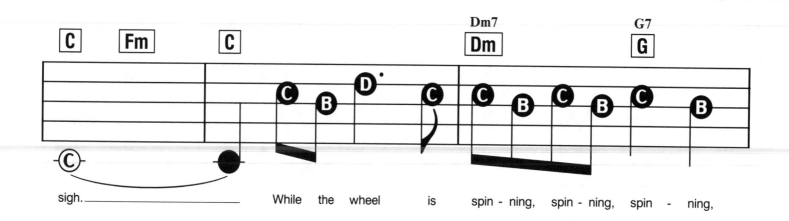

sigh._____ While the wheel is spin - ning, spin - ning, spin - ning,

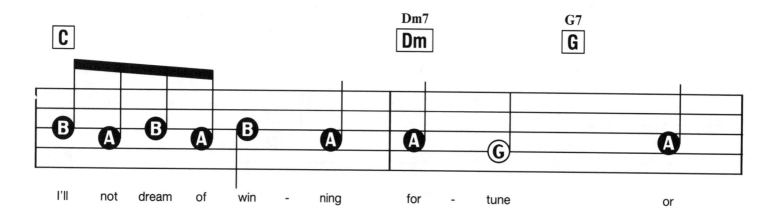

I'll not dream of win - ning for - tune or

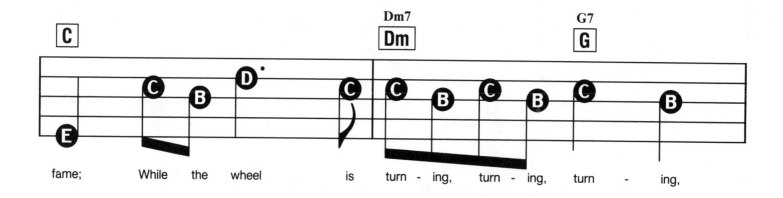

fame; While the wheel is turn - ing, turn - ing, turn - ing,

# Wheel Of Fortune

Registration 9
Rhythm: Swing

Words and Music by
Bennie Benjamin and George Weiss

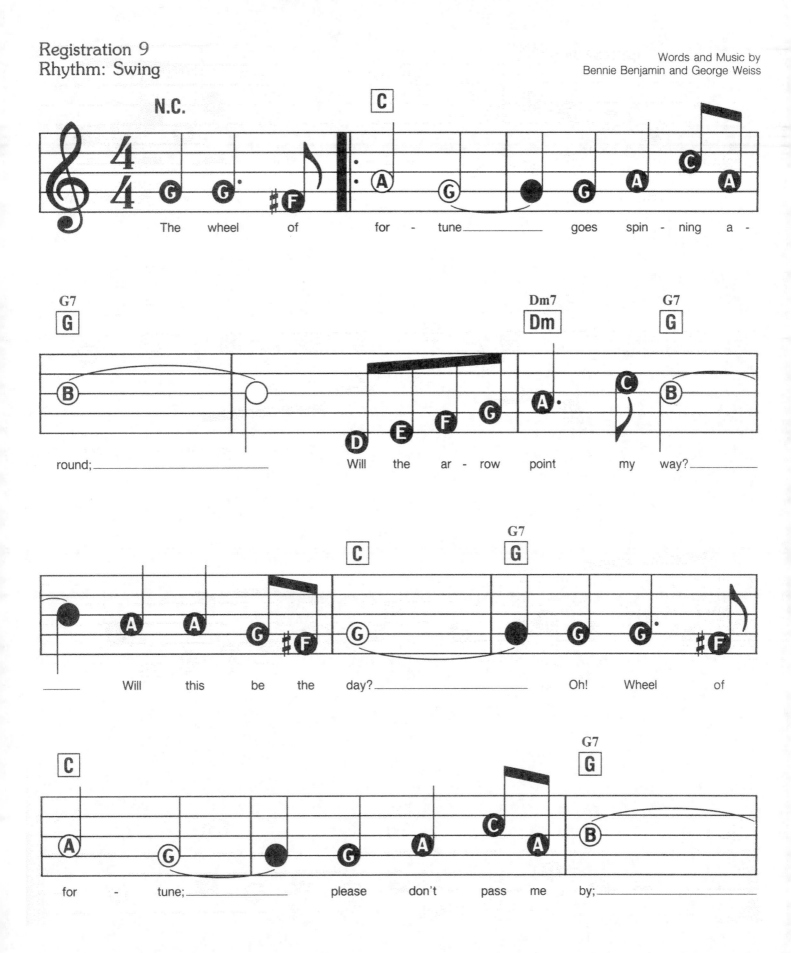

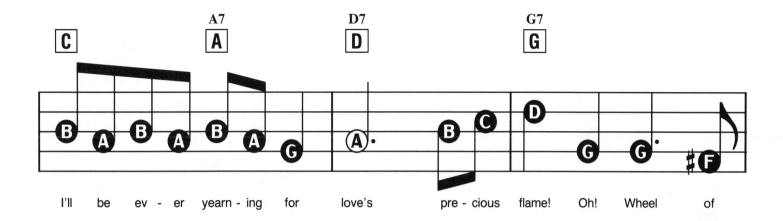

I'll be ev - er yearn - ing for love's pre - cious flame! Oh! Wheel of

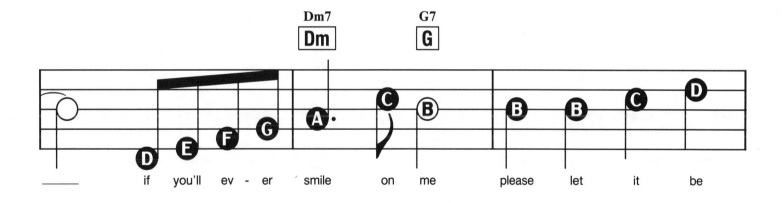

for - tune,_____ I'm hop - ing some - how_____

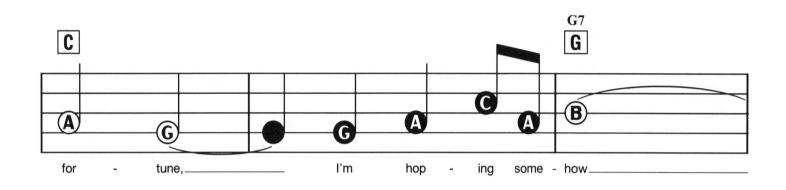

_____ if you'll ev - er smile on me please let it be

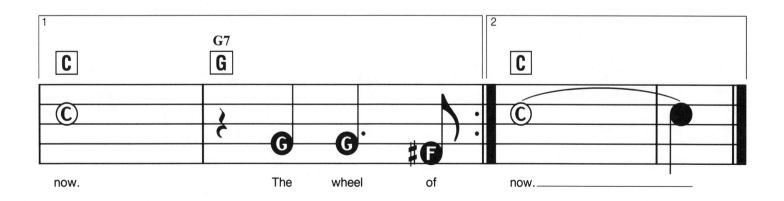

now.                    The wheel of now._____

# Three Coins In The Fountain

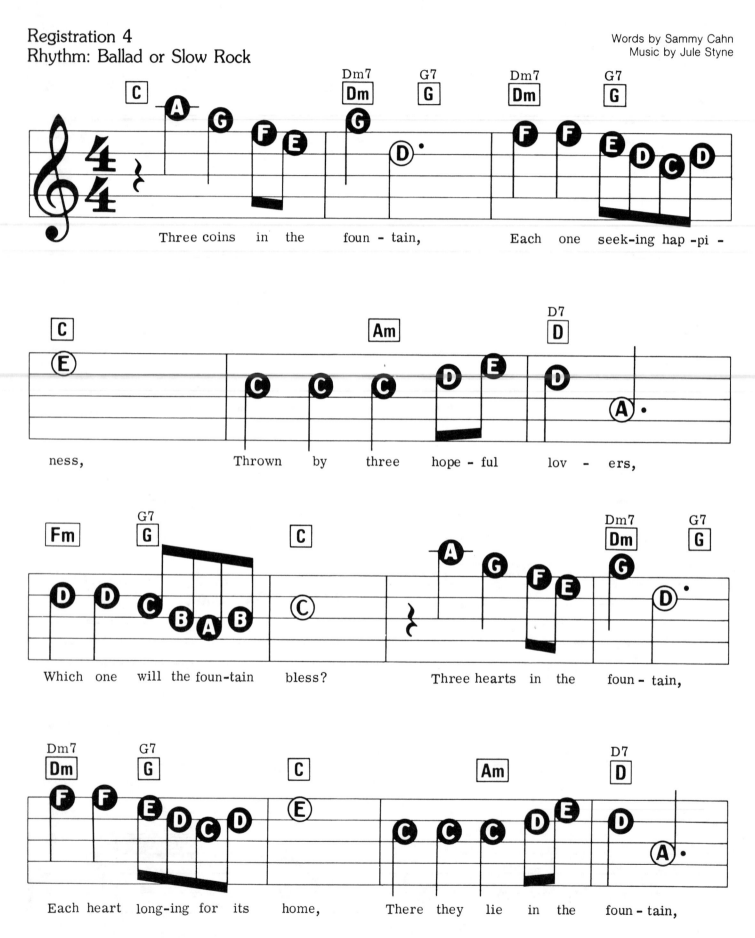

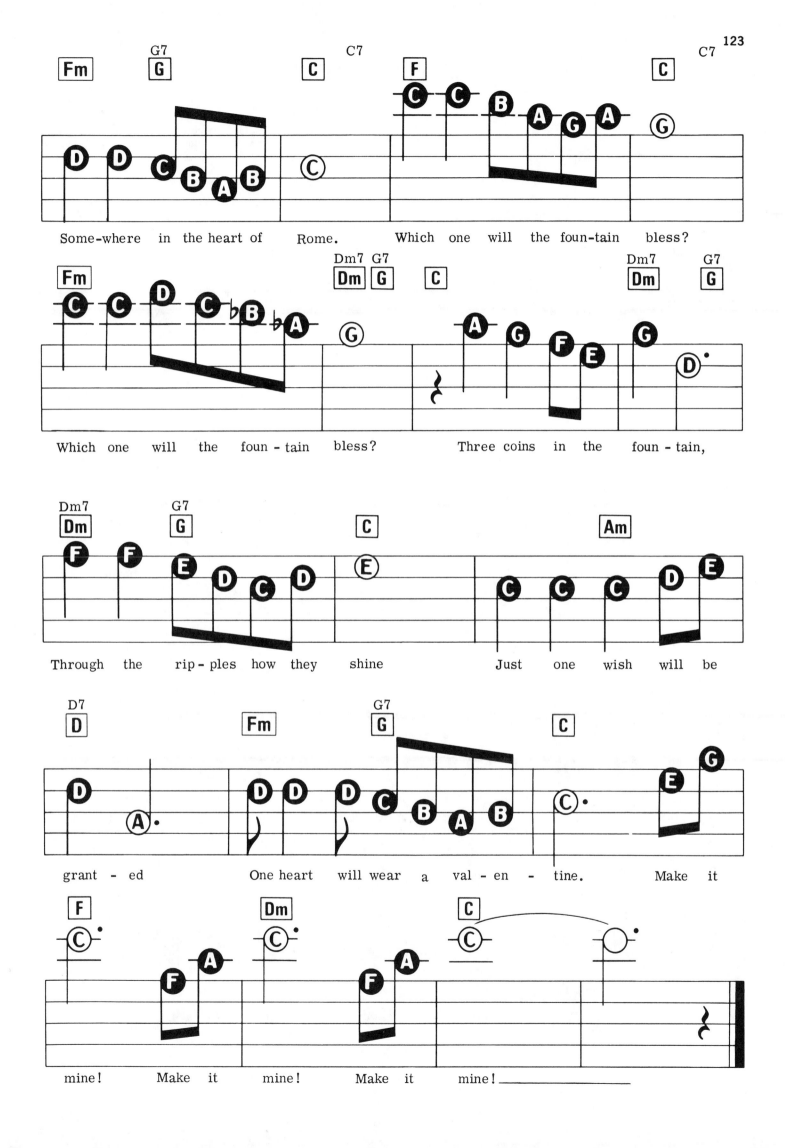

# Tom Dooley

Registration 8
Rhythm: Ballad or Slow Rock

Words and Music collected, adapted and arranged by
Frank Warner, John A. Lomax and Alan Lomax
From the singing of Frank Proffitt

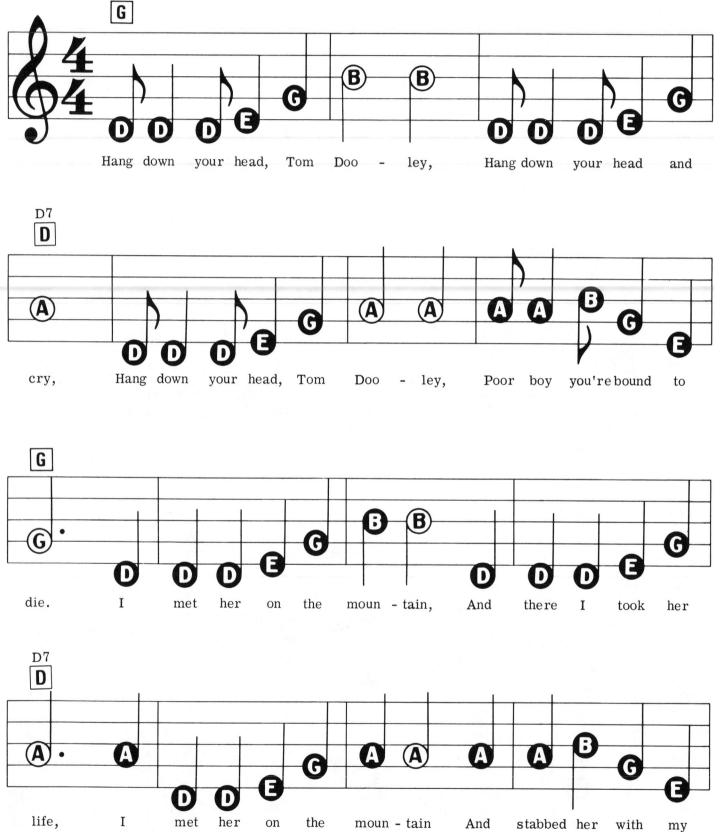

# True Love

Registration 4
Rhythm: Waltz

Words and Music by
Cole Porter

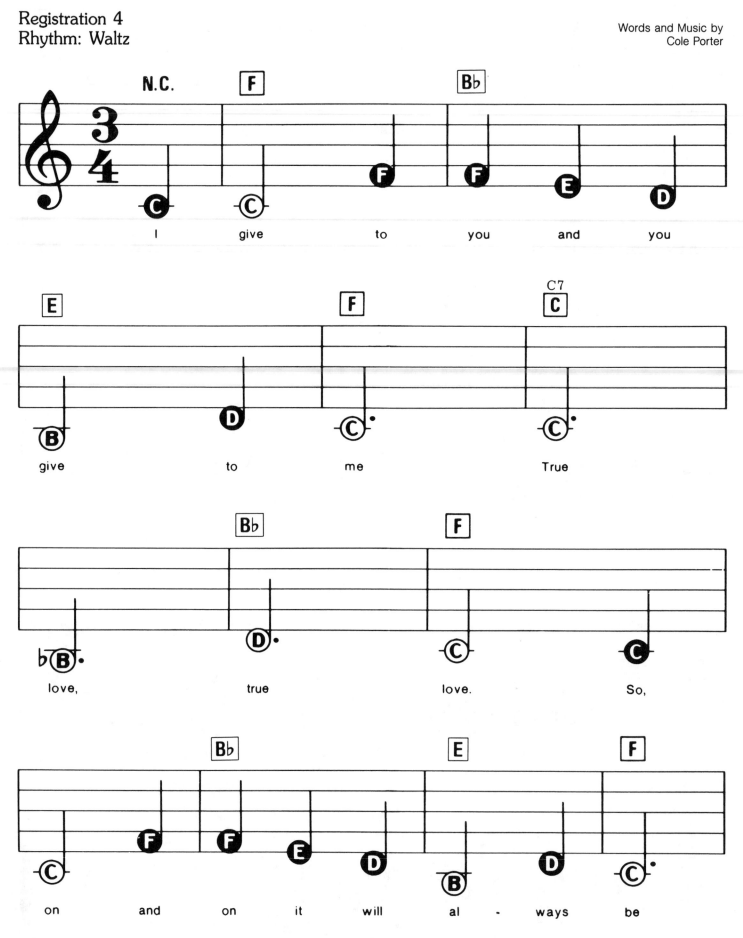

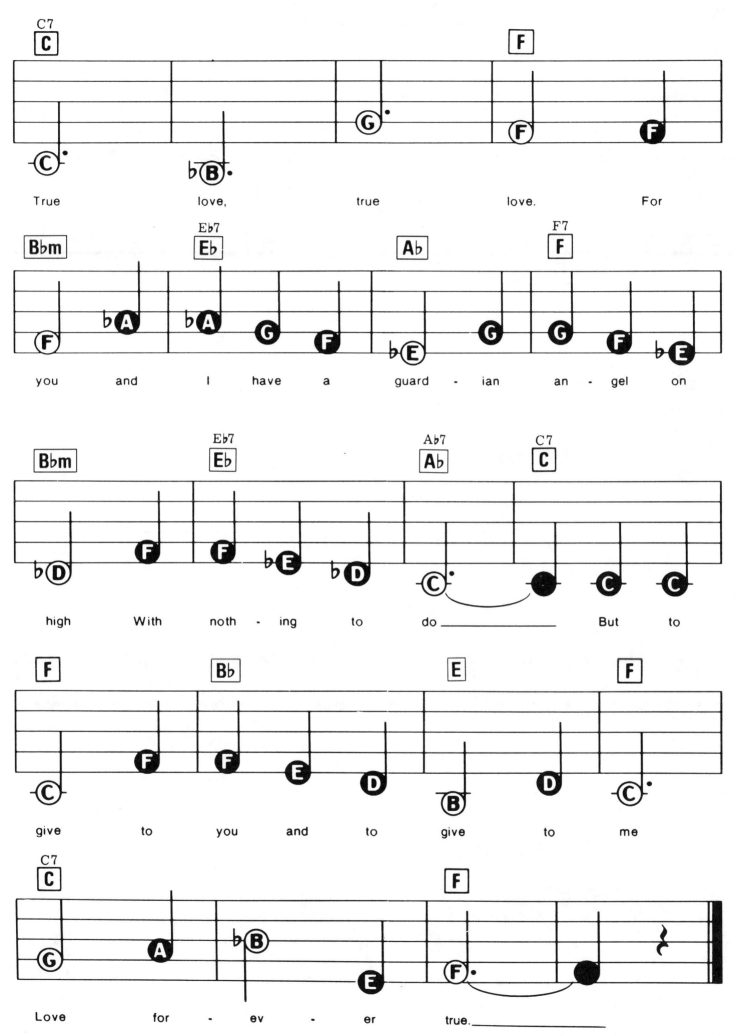

# Unforgettable

Registration 3
Rhythm: Fox Trot or Swing

Words and Music by
Irving Gordon

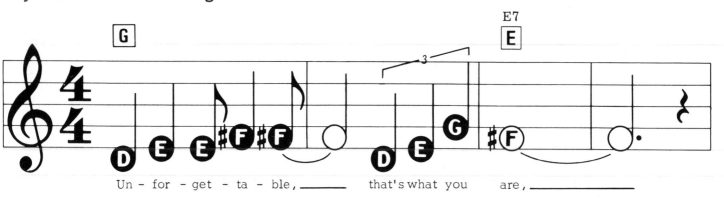

Un - for - get - ta - ble, _____ that's what you are, _____

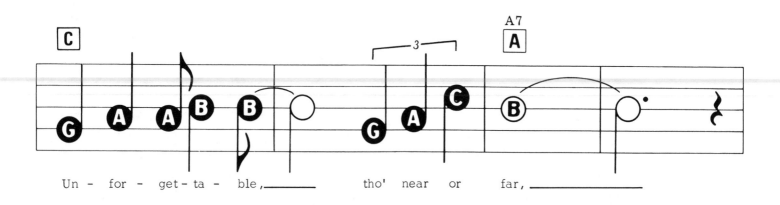

Un - for - get - ta - ble, _____ tho' near or far, _____

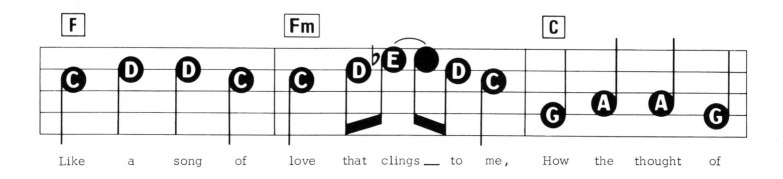

Like a song of love that clings __ to me, How the thought of

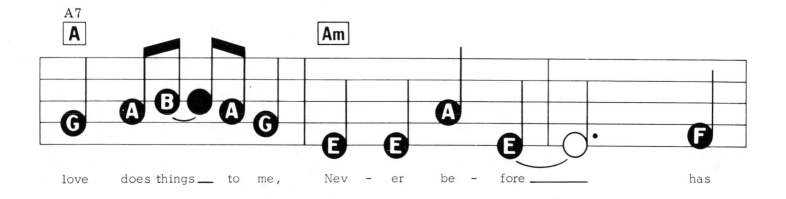

love does things __ to me, Nev - er be - fore _____ has

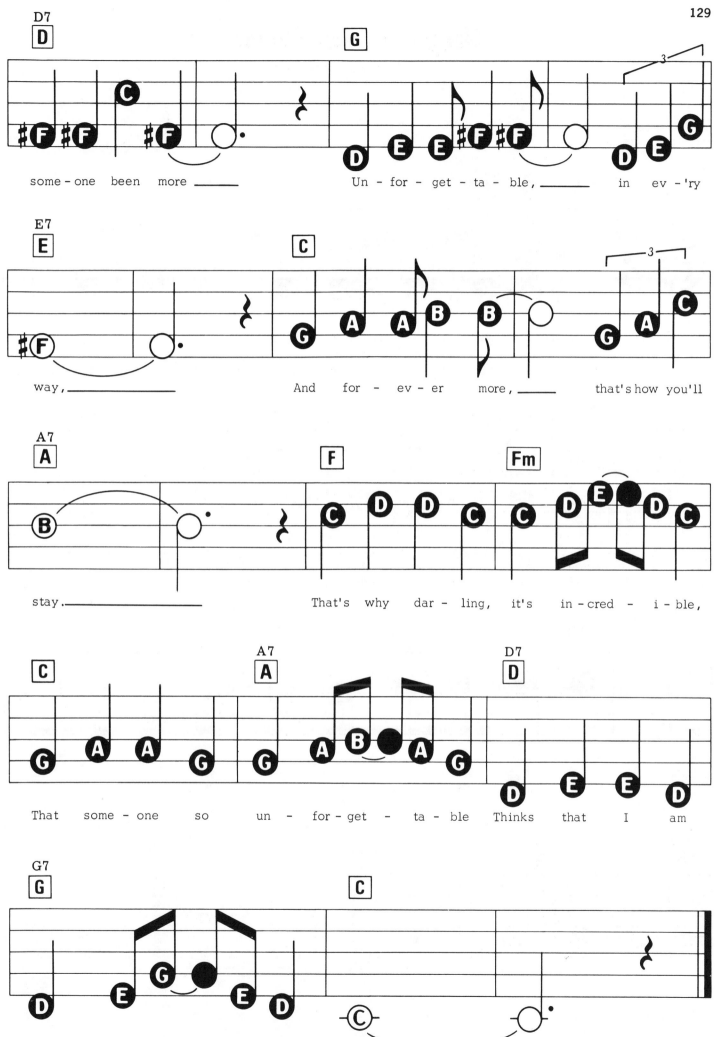

# Vaya Con Dios
### (May God Be With You)

Registration 2
Rhythm: Waltz

Words and Music by Larry Russell,
Inez James and Buddy Pepper

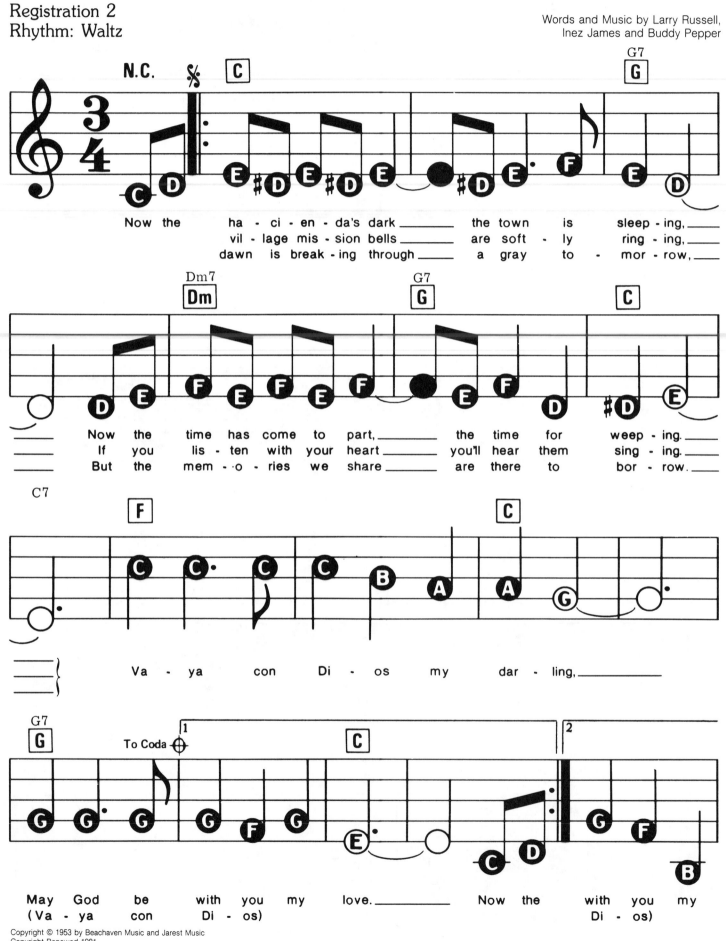

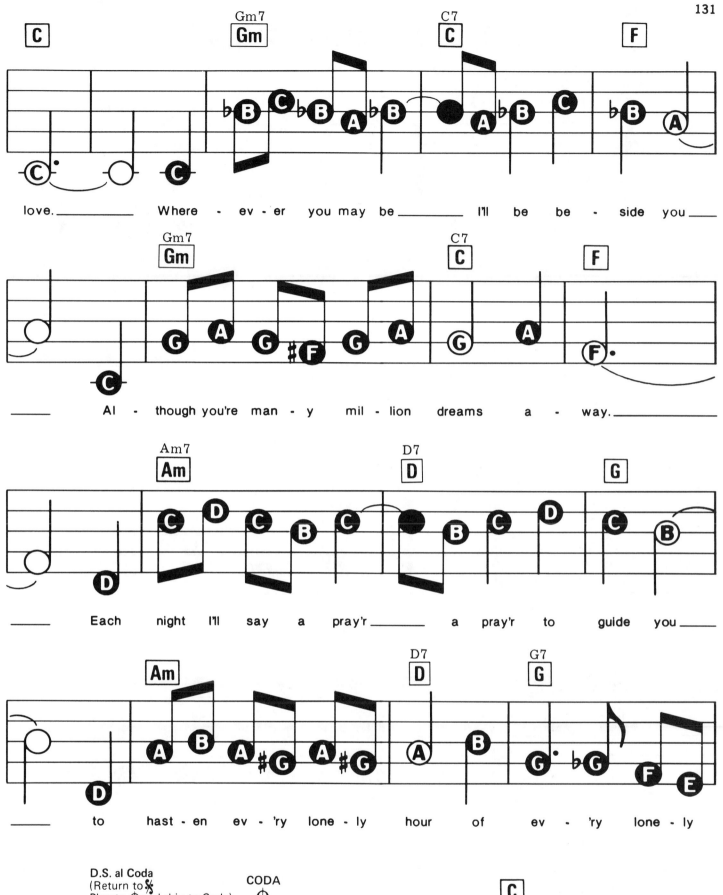

love._____ Where - ev - er you may be _____ I'll be be - side you _____

\_\_\_\_\_ Al - though you're man - y mil - lion dreams a - way.\_\_\_\_\_

\_\_\_\_\_ Each night I'll say a pray'r \_\_\_\_\_ a pray'r to guide you \_\_\_\_\_

\_\_\_\_\_ to hast - en ev - 'ry lone - ly hour of ev - 'ry lone - ly

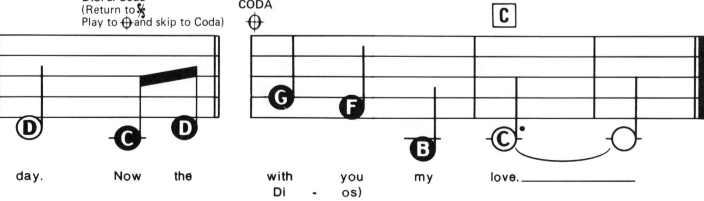

**D.S. al Coda**
(Return to %
Play to ⊕ and skip to Coda)

CODA ⊕

day. Now the

with you my love.\_\_\_\_\_
(Di - os)

# The Wayward Wind

Registration 4
Rhythm: Country or Shuffle

Words and Music by
Herb Newman and Stan Lebowsky

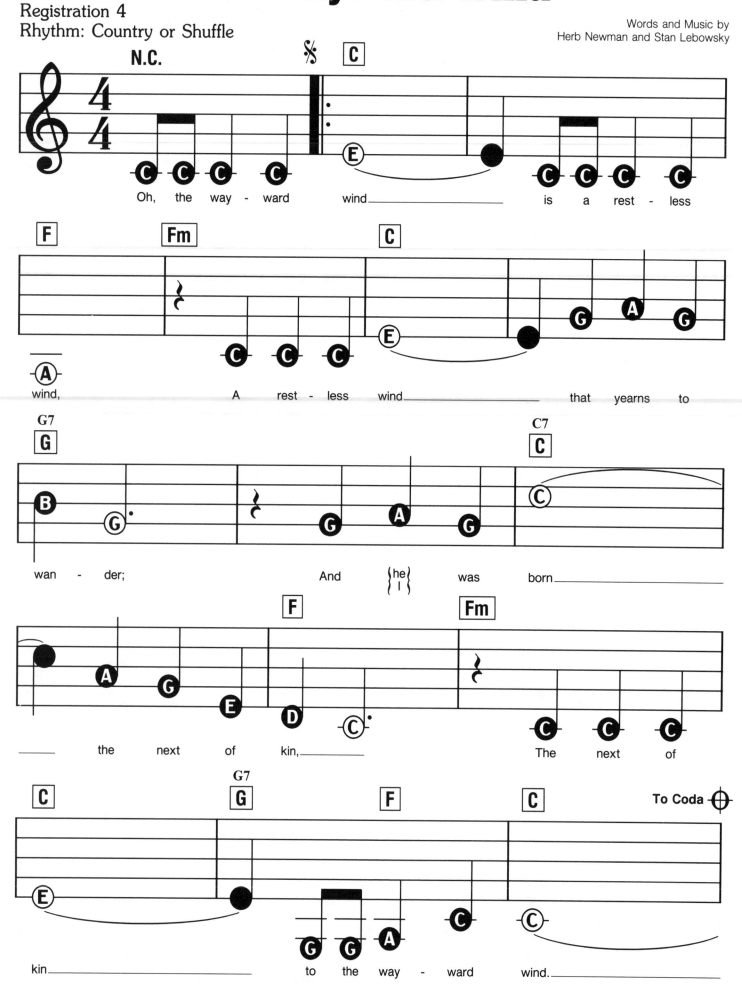

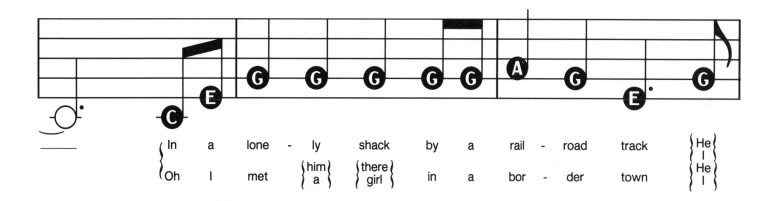

In a lone - ly shack by a rail - road track {He} {I} {He}
Oh I met {him} {a} {there} {girl} in a bor - der town {I} {He}

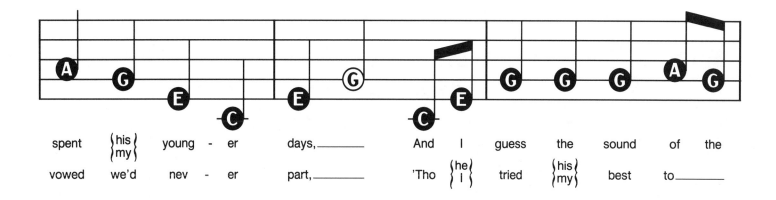

spent {his} {my} young - er days, _____ And I guess the sound of the
vowed we'd nev - er part, _____ 'Tho {he} {I} tried {his} {my} best to _____

G7

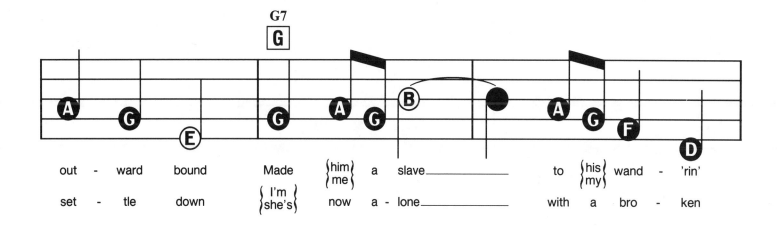

out - ward bound Made {him} {me} a slave _____ to {his} {my} wand - 'rin'
set - tle down {I'm} {she's} now a - lone _____ with a bro - ken

**2nd time D.S. al Coda**
(Return to 𝄋
Play to ⊕ and
skip to Coda)

**CODA**

C

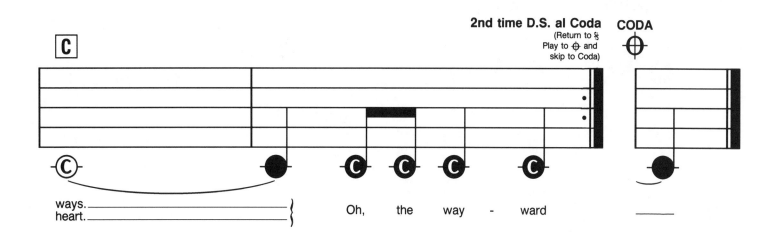

ways. _____
heart. _____ } Oh, the way - ward _____

# When I Fall In Love

Registration 10
Rhythm: Fox Trot or Ballad

Words by Edward Heyman
Music by Victor Young

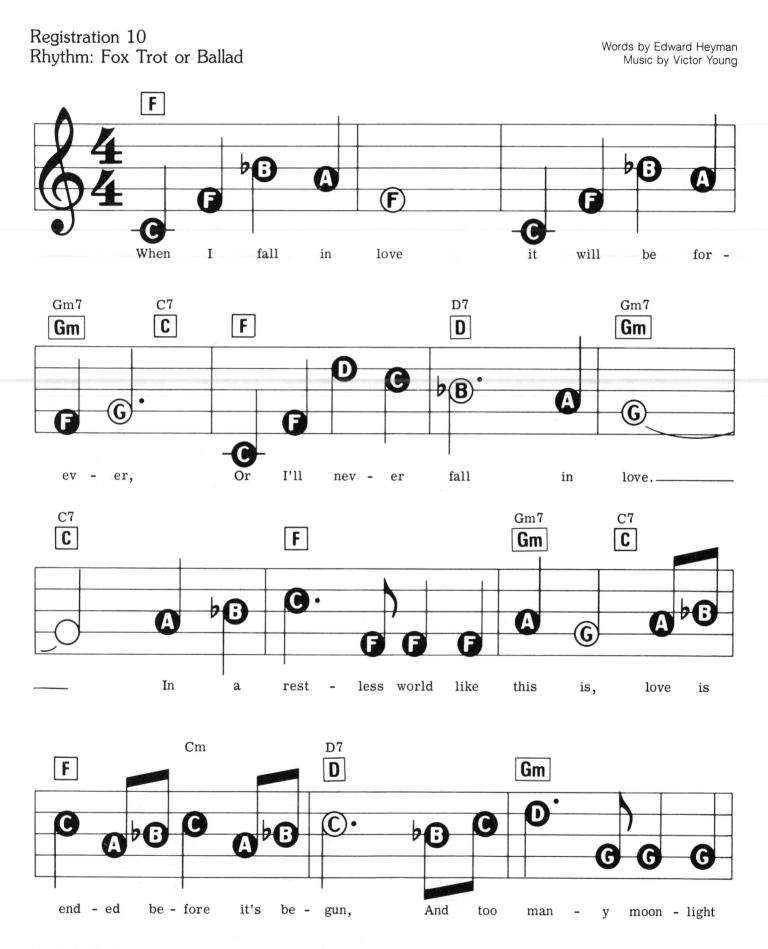

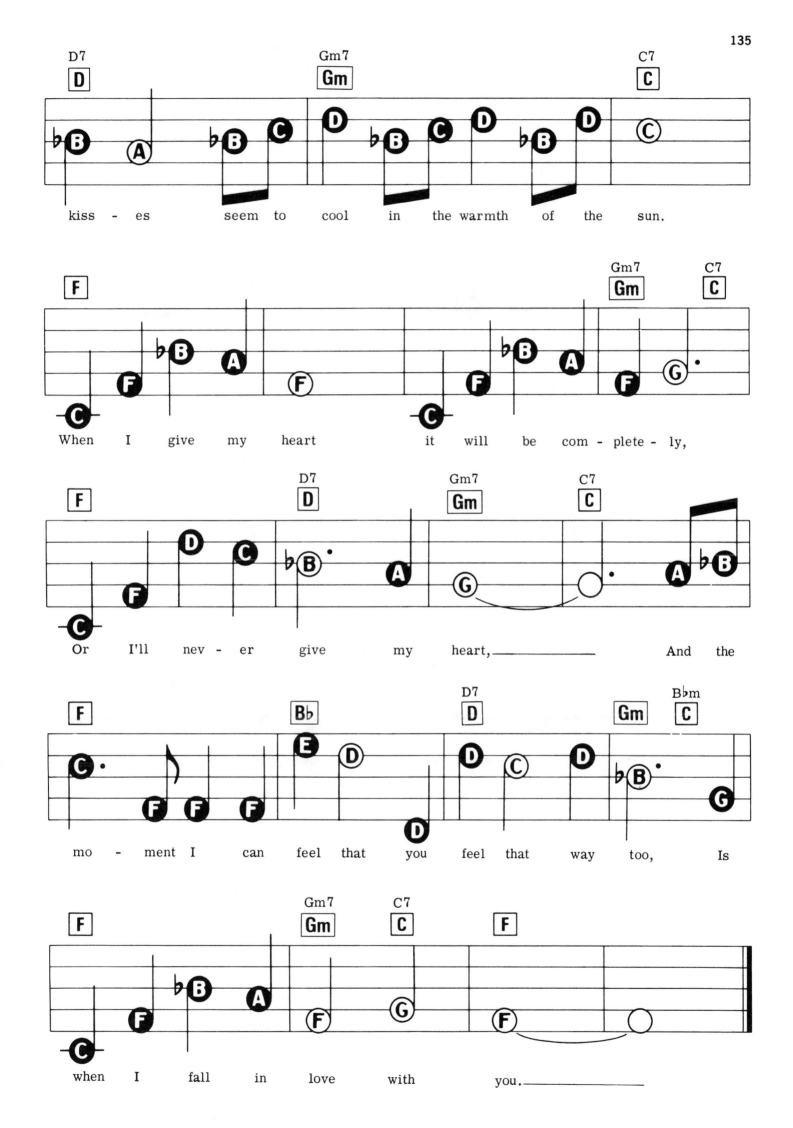

# Wonderful! Wonderful!

Registration 10
Rhythm: Ballad or Fox Trot

Words by Ben Raleigh
Music by Sherman Edwards

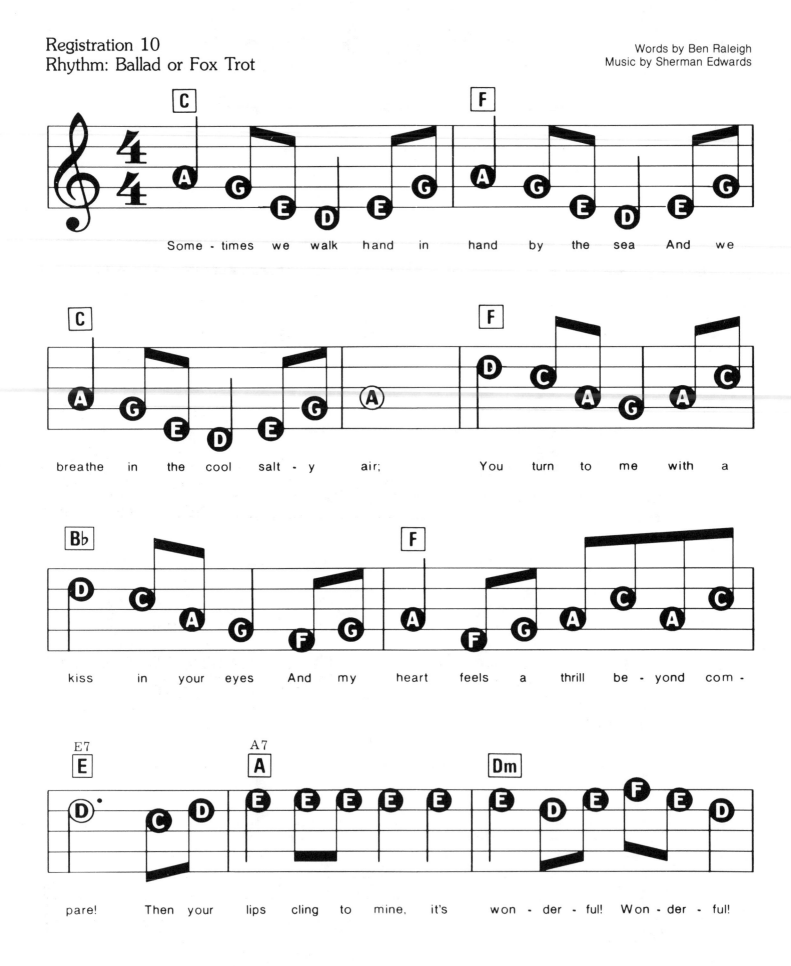

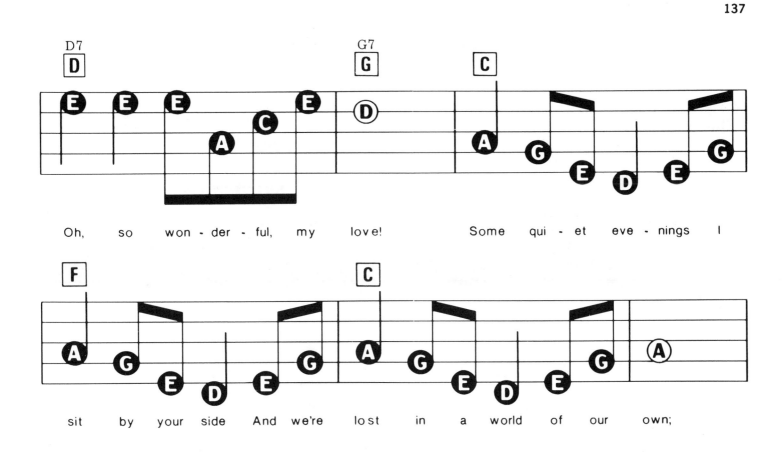

Oh, so won - der - ful, my love! Some qui - et eve - nings I

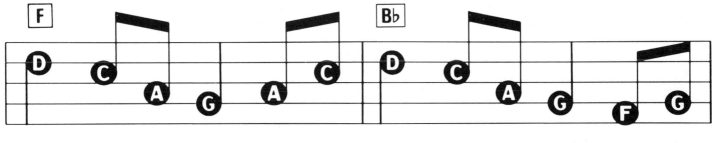

sit by your side And we're lost in a world of our own;

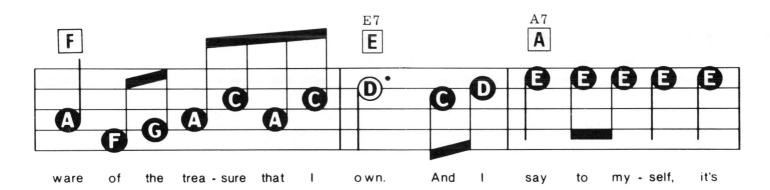

I feel the glow of your un - spo - ken love, I'm a

ware of the trea - sure that I own. And I say to my - self, it's

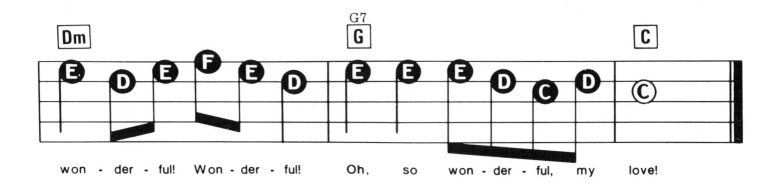

won - der - ful! Won - der - ful! Oh, so won - der - ful, my love!

# Young At Heart

Registration 3
Rhythm: Fox Trot

Words by Carolyn Leigh
Music by Johnny Richards

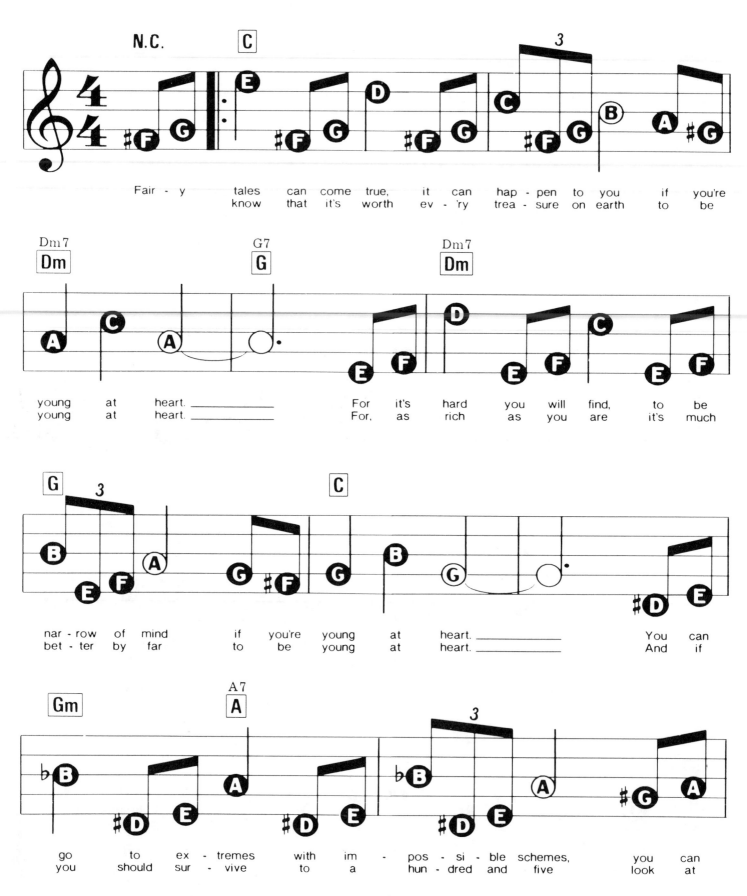

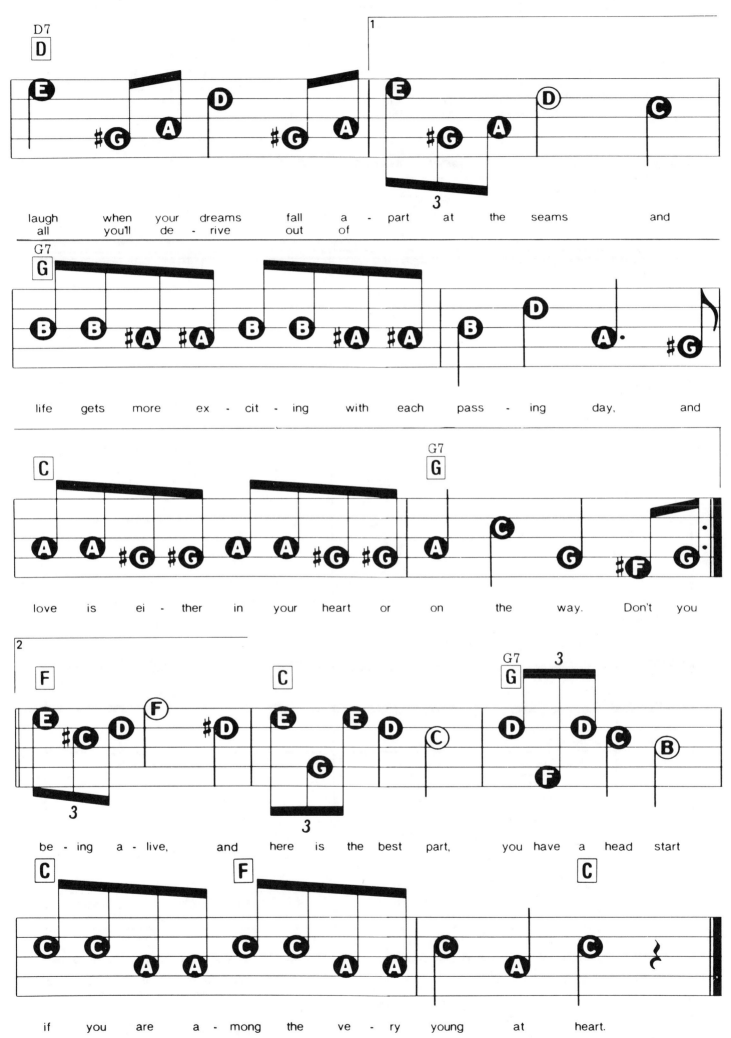

laugh when your dreams fall a - part at the seams and
all you'll de - rive out of

life gets more ex - cit - ing with each pass - ing day, and

love is ei - ther in your heart or on the way. Don't you

be - ing a - live, and here is the best part, you have a head start

if you are a - mong the ve - ry young at heart.

# E-Z Play® TODAY Registration Guide
## For All Organs

On the following chart are 10 numbered registrations for both tonebar (TB) and electronic tab organs. The numbers correspond to the registration numbers on the E-Z Play TODAY songs. Set up as many voices and controls listed for each specific number as you have available on your instrument. For more detailed registrations, ask your dealer for the E-Z Play TODAY Registration Guide for your particular organ model.

| REG. NO. | | UPPER (SOLO) | LOWER (ACCOMPANIMENT) | PEDAL | GENERALS |
|---|---|---|---|---|---|
| 1 | Tab | Flute 16', 2' | Diapason 8'<br>Flute 4' | Flute 16', 8' | Tremolo/Leslie – Fast |
| 1 | TB | 80 0808 000 | (00) 7600 000 | 46, Sustain | Tremolo/Leslie – Fast (Upper/Lower) |
| 2 | Tab | Flute 16', 8', 4', 2', 1' | Diapason 8'<br>Flute 8', 4' | Flute 16'<br>String 8' | Tremolo/Leslie – Fast |
| 2 | TB | 80 7806 004 | (00) 7503 000 | 46, Sustain | Tremolo/Leslie – Fast (Upper/Lower) |
| 3 | Tab | Flute 8', 4', 2⅔', 2'<br>String 8', 4' | Diapason 8'<br>Flute 4'<br>String 8' | Flute 16', 8' | Tremolo/Leslie – Fast |
| 3 | TB | 40 4555 554 | (00) 7503 333 | 46, Sustain | Tremolo/Leslie – Fast (Upper/Lower) |
| 4 | Tab | Flute 16', 8', 4'<br>Reed 16', 8' | Flute 8', (4)<br>Reed 8' | Flute 8'<br>String 8' | Tremolo/Leslie – Fast |
| 4 | TB | 80 7766 008 | (00) 7540 000 | 54, Sustain | Tremolo/Leslie – Fast (Upper/Lower) |
| 5 | Tab | Flute 16', 4', 2'<br>Reed 16', 8'<br>String 8', 4' | Diapason 8'<br>Reed 8'<br>String 4' | Flute 16', 8'<br>String 8' | Tremolo/Leslie |
| 5 | TB | 40 4555 554<br>Add all 4', 2' voices | (00) 7503 333 | 57, Sustain | |
| 6 | Tab | Flute 16', 8', 4'<br>Diapason 8'<br>String 8' | Diapason 8'<br>Flute 8'<br>String 4' | Diapason 8'<br>Flute 8' | Tremolo/Leslie – Slow (Chorale) |
| 6 | TB | 45 6777 643 | (00) 6604 020 | 64, Sustain | Tremolo/Leslie – Slow (Chorale) |
| 7 | Tab | Flute 16', 8',<br>5⅓', 2⅔', 1' | Flute 8', 4'<br>Reed 8' | Flute 8'<br>String 8' | Chorus (optional)<br>Perc Attack |
| 7 | TB | 88 0088 000 | (00) 4333 000 | 45, Sustain | Tremolo/Leslie – Slow (Chorale) |
| 8 | Tab | Piano Preset or<br>Flute 8' or<br>Diapason 8' | Diapason 8' | Flute 8' | |
| 8 | TB | 00 8421 000 | (00) 4302 010 | 43, Sustain | Perc Piano |
| 9 | Tab | Clarinet Preset<br>or Flute 8'<br>Reed 16', 8' | Flute 8'<br>Reed 8' | Flute 16', 8' | Vibrato |
| 9 | TB | 00 8080 840 | (00) 5442 000 | 43, Sustain | Vibrato |
| 10 | Tab | String (Violin) Preset<br>or Flute 16'<br>String 8', 4' | Flute 8'<br>Reed 8' | Flute 16', 8' | Vibrato or Delayed Vibrato |
| 10 | TB | 00 7888 888 | (00) 7765 443 | 57, Sustain | Vibrato or Delayed Vibrato |

NOTE: TIBIAS may be used in place of FLUTES. VIBRATO may be used in place of LESLIE.

## KEYBOARD ALPHABETICAL SONGFINDER

Complete listing of over 3000 songs included in the E-Z Play TODAY Songbook Series, SOLO TODAY, ORGAN ADVENTURE, EASY ELECTRONIC KEYBOARD MUSIC and PORTABLE KEYBOARD MUSIC Series. Song titles are cross-referenced to the books in which they can be found.

Available free of charge from your local music store. Or, write to:

HAL LEONARD PUBLISHING CORP.
P.O. Box 13819, Milwaukee, WI 53213

Ask for #90500057.

THE ENJOYMENT YOU'VE RECEIVED WITH THIS E-Z PLAY TODAY SONG-BOOK CAN NOW BE EXPANDED INTO EVEN MORE FUN AND ACCOMPLISHMENT WHEN YOU STEP UP TO THE SOLO TODAY SERIES. SOLO TODAY'S UNIQUE NOTATION SYSTEM INTRODUCES YOU, STEP BY STEP, TO READING AND PLAYING CONVENTIONAL TWO-STAFF NOTATION WITH THE SAME FUN AND EASE YOU FOUND IN E-Z PLAY TODAY SONGBOOKS

## INTRODUCTORY BOOKS

### STEP BY STEP — BOOK A
The first introductory book to the SOLO TODAY series teaches the fundamentals of music and bass clef note reading in a comprehensive, yet easy-to-understand format. The ideal way to learn and enjoy playing conventional music notation.
00106965.......................................$5.95

### STEP BY STEP — BOOK B
This book adds the finishing touches to your learning and playing needs for SOLO TODAY. More reading experience, double notes, pedal patterns plus the "extras" to keep your keyboard enjoyment high.
00106966.......................................$5.95

## CONTINUE YOUR MUSICAL ENJOYMENT WITH THESE
## SOLO TODAY SONGBOOKS

### 1. COUNTRY POTPOURRI
Country music at its best. 20 hits, including: Heartaches By The Number • King Of The Road • Kiss An Angel Good Mornin' • Make The World Go Away • Tennessee Waltz • and more.
00106500.............................................................$6.95

### 2. TOP REQUESTS
20 standards, including: Autumn Leaves • Hello, Dolly! • Mame • Sentimental Journey • Tenderly • and more.
00107000.............................................................$6.95

### 3. INSPIRATIONAL HYMNS
A distinctive religious collection of 20 songs, including: Holy, Holy, Holy • Love Lifted Me • Only Trust Him • Revive Us Again • We Gather Together • and more.
00106700.............................................................$6.95

### 5. SONGS OF CHRISTMAS
A collection of 20 Christmas favorites, including Styling Tips on creating chimes and sleigh bells: Blue Christmas • The Christmas Song • Home For The Holidays • Little Drummer Boy • Sleigh Ride and more.
0010106950..............................................................$6.95

### 6. A CLASSIC AFFAIR
16 of the world's best loved classical melodies, along with Styling Tips on creating expression: Andante Cantabile • Brahm's Lullaby • March From "The Nutcracker Suite" • To A Wild Rose • Two Guitars • and more.
00106450........................................$6.95

### 7. FANFARE
16 timeless musical hits, along with Styling Tips on creating introductions: Do-Re-Mi • Getting To Know You • It Might As Well Be Spring • I Whistle A Happy Tune • Oh, What A Beautiful Mornin' • and more.
00106600........................................$6.95

### 8. IT'S COUNTRY
15 top country selections, along with Styling Tips on creating country playing techniques: Born To Lose • Heartbreaker • Sail Away • San Antonio Rose • You Needed Me • and more.
00106720........................................$6.95

### 9. CONTEMPORARY HITS
A selection of 13 of the best, including: Can't Smile Without You • Endless Love • Hello Again • Islands In The Stream • Memory • and more.
00106492........................................$6.95

### 10. SOLID GOLD
16 top hits from recent years, including: Arthur's Theme • Chariots Of Fire • Nine To Five • The Rose • Up Where We Belong • The Way We Were • and more.
00106938........................................$6.95

### 11. SUPER POPS
13 songs from the top of the charts, including: Could've Been • She's Like The Wind • Somewhere Out There • What A Wonderful World • and more.
00106980.............................................................$6.95

### 12. DISNEY FAVORITES
14 songs, including: Candle On The Water • It's A Small World • Once Upon A Dream • Winnie The Pooh • Zip-A-Dee-Doo-Dah • and more.
00106540.............................................................$6.95

### 13. RODGERS AND HAMMERSTEIN
16 songs, including: Climb Every Mountain • If I Loved You • Oklahoma! • Shall We Dance • The Sound Of Music • You'll Never Walk Alone • and more.
00106905.............................................................$6.95

*For more information, see your local music dealer, or write to:*

Hal Leonard Publishing Corporation
P.O. Box 13819 Milwaukee, Wisconsin 53213